An Introduction to
INFORMATION PROCESSING AND RETRIEVAL
(For Library and Information Professionals)

An Introduction to INFORMATION PROCESSING AND RETRIEVAL

(For Library and Information Professionals)

By

N. R. Satyanarayana

Formerly, Professor of Library and Information Science

University of Lucknow

Ess Ess Publications

New Delhi

An Introduction to
INFORMATION PROCESSING AND RETRIEVAL
(For Library and Information Professionals)

ISBN: 978-81-7000-813-2

First Published 2016

Published by:
Ess Ess Publications
4831/24, Ansari Road,
Darya Ganj,
New Delhi-110 002.
INDIA
Phones: 23260807, 41563444
Fax: 41563334
E-mail: info@essessreference.com
www.essessreference.com

Cover Design by *Patch Creative Unit*

Printed and bound in India at Salasar Imaging Systems.

Contents

Preface

The process of handling cumulative human knowledge to the succeeding generations either by word of mouth or in the graphic form is of paramount importance for further development of knowledge itself. The very existence of written records demands that they should be listed and their existence is acknowledged. If this listing is done in a systematic manner, we can have some bibliographical control over the ever expanding and multi dimensional graphic knowledge and put it in use for further human development.

Information thus generated by the producers of knowledge is ultimately to be communicated to the user community for consumption and further expansion. Socio-economic development of a nation depends on it. Librarians and information workers occupy a pivotal position in the communication triangle. He acts as a middleman between the creator of knowledge and consumer of information. Information Storage and Retrieval System is an important operational tool, which this middleman uses in discharging his responsibilities.

An information retrieval system is designed to retrieve (call-back) the documents or information required by the users community. Ideally there would have been no need for establishing such a system if the number of documents in the universe would not have exceeded a few hundreds, and if each author would have known the reader of his document. In this case he could have sent the material directly to the reader. Unfortunately, it is not true and quite a few other reasons are there which have made the society bound to establish Information Processing and Retrieval System to facilitate the channelization of information from the author to the readers, and thus, to facilitate the growth of knowledge. Thus, Information Processing and Retrieval System aims to collect, organize and provide all the documents to the user as soon as required.

For quite some time there has been a felt need for a suitable and comprehensive book on Information Processing and Retrieval, covering theoretical and practical aspects of the subjects for the students of library and information science as also for the working librarians and professionals. The present work is a modest endeavour in this direction.

An attempt has been made here to present an integrated view of the subject of Information Processing and Retrieval. However, this work does not purport to be a compendium but tries to give an introduction to the subject about them. In order to keep this work relevant and efficient many ideas had to be omitted. The purpose has been mainly to help in the creation of such a tool, that helps in making information available and thus provide an effective communication link between the sources and seekers of information.

During the preparation of this volume the author has taken the help of Mr. Samant Gupta and Ms. Smriti Srivastava. The author sincerely thank them. M/S Ess Ess Publications, New Delhi, especially Mr. Sumit Sethi, deserves special thanks for bringing this volume in this presentable format.

Lucknow **N.R. Satyanarayana**

Sri Rama Navami, 2005

Part I
Introduction

1

Introduction to Information Processing

By nature man is social and the society is the web of social relationship. Being a social animal, man wants to communicate as among all animals, only man is endowed with the gift of speech.

From time immemorial, man has used various means for communicating his ideas, his feelings, his beliefs, his faith, his ethos and pathos with his fellow beings. He communicates by gestures, facial expressions, grunts and cries, which can very effectively communicate emotions. Man also communicates through figures, pictures, visuals, mathematical and scientific signs and symbols, music, dance and above all by the all powerful words both spoken and written.

In the beginning, we are told it was words and words alone. Without "word", indeed, there could be no beginning. Prehistoric man grouped his tortuous journey to the historic man when he started sharing his experiences and thoughts with his fellow beings. The spoken word as the unit of language has been the most laudable achievement of Homo Sapiens in developing complex societies. If speech was the first step forward in the development of human communication, the second great milestone was invention of writing. By virtue of writing, history could be recorded permanently and in detail, technical discoveries could be handed on, and records of every kind could be kept.

In the light of material and the demand of the society at the particular juncture of the human history, the man had been developing methods of recording his experiences through clay - tablets, wax - tablets, papyrus sheets, parchment roles, codices, etc. The third great leap forward came with invention of printing, by means of which what was written could be reproduced and distributed in quantity, thus disseminating information and learning among ever widening circles of the community. Bewildering amount of progress have accompanied the development of electronic systems of communication- the telegraph, telephone and especially radio - television and satellites. Recently, the electronic computer and telecommunication technologies have brought many other revolutionary possibilities.

All societies- ancient, medieval or modern- have functioned and prospered on the basis of information and knowledge in their various stages of developments. In the past, the creation of new knowledge, new innovations and new inventions have been the efforts of a small number of individuals with a passion for and dedication to such activities and, therefore, growth of new knowledge has largely been solo, sporadic and incidental. Application of new information and knowledge was largely accidental; consequently, progress in terms of material advancement of life had been slow. But from the beginning of this century, more particularly in the last half of the century, information has come to occupy the central position, to be reckoned as a driving force for all human development. Information and knowledge are therefore, deliberately being created to meet a variety of challenges posed to human living. Let us examine the causes for such a reckoning.

PIVOTAL ROLE OF INFORMATION TODAY

Some of the factors attributed to the current value of information and knowledge that have greatly contributed to the socio-economic development are:

- Research and Development (R & D)
- Education, Training and Skill development
- Government affairs
- Industry and Business; and
- Mass Communication

Organization means arrangement of ideas and objects in a systematic order. It pervades various activities of our life. Without it, human progress would be impossible. Bibliographic organization is a means of communication, which is concerned with the organization and control of publications. The function of bibliographic organization is to ensure that documents are adequately published, housed and recorded; its purpose is the efficient identification, selection, and location of these documents as required.

An information retrieval system is designed to retrieve the documents or information required by the users community. Ideally, there would not have been any need for establishing such a system if the number of documents in the universe would not have exceeded a few hundreds or so, and if each author in each subject field would have known the reader of his document, in this case he could have sent the material directly to the reader. Unfortunately, none of these is true and quite a few other reasons are there which have made the society bound to establish information retrieval systems to facilitate the channelization of information from the author to the readers, and thus, to facilitate the growth of knowledge. Thus, an information retrieval system aims at collecting and organizing all the documents available in one or more subject areas in order to provide them to the user as soon as required.

An information retrieval system serves as a link

between authors and the world of readers. Authors express their ideas in documents. There are always some readers who wants to know them but do not know how to reach them. Information retrieval matches the requirements of the readers with the knowledge created by the authors.

IS BIBLIOGRAPHIC ORGANIZATION DIFFICULT ?

There are many reasons why bibliographic organisation and control is becoming increasingly difficult. Some of the reasons are:

(i) Number of documents : In a conservative estimate, nowadays almost thirty thousand books are published annually by the British Book Trade alone; and it is further estimated that there are over 1,00,000 periodicals in science and technology; over 90,000 articles on chemistry are now abstracted each year by Chemical Abstracts.

(ii) The language of documents : Several important documents are published in an increasing number of languages as developing countries are producing more literature. The language barrier restricts free flow of documents among the countries of the world.

(iii) Problem of scattering : In addition to the problem of proliferation of published literature, there is also the problem of scattering i.e., the literature of a subject is widely scattered in a number of publications like journals, patents, standards, conference proceeding etc.

(iv) Complexity of publications : The development of non-conventional methods of printing has facilitated publication by various organizations, which are not from the book trade. Such publications are often missed by national bibliographies and reviewing sources and consequently are less easily controlled.

(v) Need for secondary periodicals : With the tremendous proliferation of published literature, with all its complexities of multiplicity and sources and diversity of forms and languages. Hence, various types of tools and techniques have been evolved to keep scientists informed of current and retrospective literature like indexing and abstracting services, which are perhaps the most important and useful amongst all these tools.

Some of the important information retrieval techniques are briefly mentioned below and elaborated for easy understanding.

CLASSIFICATION

Classification pervades all the various activities of our life. It helps in converting unorganized thoughts and impressions into recognizable patterns. The term classes was used to refer to a group of persons possessing certain qualities in common, as well as belonging to the same class.

Library classification is related to arrangement of books and other documents in a systematic, helpful and permanent order. It aims to create a system out of disorder, and provide a comprehensive view of the documents on a subject or a group of subjects. Once an orderly arrangement has been achieved, then it will save the time of successive readers as well as librarian. In the choice of a suitable criterion for arrangement, the following qualities may be kept in view:

1. The number of groups formed should be large enough;
2. Each group should include a large number of documents;
3. The grouping should be helpful;
4. The grouping achieved should be permanent in nature; and
5. Each group should be meaningful.

CATALOGUING

Cataloguing and classification are two interrelated processes performed in a library, whose basic purpose is to aid users in locating and selecting appropriate library materials required for their study and research. To a large extent, these two processes are complementary and supplementary to each other. Library catalogue is "a list of documents in a library or in a collection forming a portion of it".

Objectives of a library catalogue were broadly described by C.A. Cutter as far back in 1876 and they are found valid and relevant even now. These are:

1. To enable a person to find a book of which
   a. the author is known, or
   b. the title is known, or
   c. the subject is known
2. To show what the library has
   a. by a given author
   b. on a given subject
   c. in a given kind of literature
3. To assist in the choice of a book
   a. as to its edition (bibliographically)
   b. as to its character (literary or topical)

An entry is a certain amount of information recorded for a specific purpose, several entries provided for a document in a library catalogue, one entry is called 'Main Entry' and the remaining entries are called 'Added' or 'Additional Entries'. Main Entry is the basic entry, providing all the essential information, which is useful and relevant for the document's identification. 'Added Entries' are intended to help the users to find a document when his approach to the document is different from the one that the library has preferred for its main entry. That is, the entries, which provide access points other than the **main** access point, are added entries.

INDEXING

Index is concerned with indicating an object or idea to one who does not know where that object or idea is located. The basic purpose of indexing is to help maximum of recall or retrieval of relevant information with minimum of noise. Index thus serves as an operating tool. The indexing tool becomes necessary because any store of information or documents containing information is required to be organized for repetitive use by the user. Some important functions of an index are: index provide guide to material that the user may wish to recall; to facilitate reference to the specific item; to disclose relationship; the cross references in subject indexes guide users to accepted facts of fields; and a major reason for index is to aid in solving the problem presented by many languages in which material is now published.

As there is link between a source of information and those who would have obtained some information from it, the index is necessarily a communicating link. Indexes are needed for social interaction.

ABSTRACTING

Abstracts and abstracting services have come into being as a means for controlling the prolific output of scientific research and its communication. An abstract is a brief and accurate representation of the contents of a document, in a style similar to that of the original. Abstracts are prepared in relation to the purpose of the user, the field of investigation and the intensity or depth of information required. The purpose of an abstract is : to help workers in the subject of the article to decide whether the contents of the paper are such that they desire to read it in full; to give readers for whom the paper is of 'fringe" interest as much of information as possible, so that it is necessary for them to read the whole paper; and to expedite the work of the abstracting journals by making it possible for them to reproduce immediately the author's abstract which will be of great assistance in the general improvement of information services in the scientific field.

Abstracts should contain observed facts, essential points of new method or treatment of newly designed apparatus etc. references should be made to new materials, such as new compounds, new species or varieties or forms etc. and new numerical data, such as physical constants.

THESAURUS

The word thesaurus, which has Greek origin, literally means "treasury or storehouse of knowledge". But, in modern usage, it denotes a list of terms arranged according to their relationship of ideas.

In the context of information retrieval Helen Brownson is said to be the first person who used the term "Thesaurus" in her paper presented in 1957 at the Dorking Conference on Classification Research, and Hans P. Luhn was the first person to think in terms of 'Information Retrieval Thesaurus' (IR Thesaurus). Any information retrieval system, whether manual or mechanized, requires an articulate vocabulary free from homonyms and synonyms, for its efficient functioning. An IR thesaurus fulfills this need. The main characteristics of an IR thesaurus are that: it provides descriptors to be used in indexing and retrieval; and it shows the intrinsic, semantic relationship existing between the terms.

There are also some other concepts, viz., thesaurofacet and classaurus, which possess not only all the features of a thesaurus, but also some additional features. Thesaurofacet has been developed by Jean Atchison and others for English Electric Company. It is basically a faceted classification integrated with a thesaurus.

An attempt has been made here to present an integrated view of the subject of information processing and retrieval. However, this volume gives only an introduction about them. In order to keep this work relevant and efficient many ideas had to be omitted. The purpose has been mainly to help in the creation of such a tool, which helps in making information available and thus provide an effective communication link between the sources and seekers of information.

REFERENCES

1. Chowdhury, G.G. Information Retrieval System. Calcutta : IASLIC, 1994.

2. Kemp, Alister. Knowledge Base Retrieval System. London : Aslib, 1988.

3. Khan, M.T.M. Information Organization and Communication. New Delhi: Ess Ess, 1997.

4. Lancaster, F. Wilfrid. Information Retrieval Systems: Characteristics, testing and evaluation. New York : John Wiley, 1979.

5. Oddy, R.N. [et.al.]. Information Retrieval Research. London Butterworths, 1981.

6. Vickery, B.C. Techniques of Information Retrieval. London Butterworths, 1970.

Part II

Information Storage and Retrieval System

2

Information Storage and Retrieval System : Purpose, Functions, Designing

INTRODUCTION

We may understand an information retrieval system as a system which helps us to recover information. To understand the nature of an information retrieval system, we must try to understand the meaning of its component words. Firstly, it is a system, that is composed of a set of several interacting parts (components) each of which is designed to serve a specific function for a specific purpose. All these components are interrelated to achieve a goal. Here it is to recover or retrieve information in a narrower sense, and by doing so increase the level of knowledge of the users in a broader sense. The concept of information retrieval thus pre-supposes that there are some items of information which have been organized and kept (stored) in a suitable order for an easy recovery, whenever needed.

Information storage and retrieval systems are concerned with two basic aspects: How to store information? and How to interpret its structure? Both these aspects present formidable problems for computers and equally formidable challenges for human beings involved in the process. Information retrieval thus involves finding some desired information in a store of information or a database. The basic model of ISRS is depending on the potential and actual interaction between a searcher and a database (as an information source). The searchers go for information in order to improve their knowledge for decision-making or problem-solving or for learning. By doing so they create more information by using database. On the other hand, the database producer goes on searching information with a selective basis gathers it, processes it and store the same in database in order to serve the potential demands.

DEFINITION

Information retrieval system has been defined by some specialists as under.

F.W. Lancaster defines it as "any system that is designated to facilitate the literature search activity may legitimately be called Information Retrieval System".

According to Stephen P. Harter "Information Retrieval System is a device interposed between a potential user of information and the information collection itself."

J.H. Shera defines Information Retrieval System as "a system that performs the process of locating and selecting data, relevant to a given requirement".

PURPOSE

An information retrieval system is designed to retrieve the documents or information required by the users. An information retrieval system aims at collecting and organizing all the documents available in one or more subject areas in order to provide them to users as soon as required. The following scenario shall reflect the purpose of information retrieval systems as under:

1. A writer presents a set of ideas in a document using a set of concepts.

2. Somewhere there will be some users who require the ideas but may not be able to identify those.
3. Information retrieval systems serve to match the writer's ideas expressed in the document with the user's requirements or demands for those.

Thus, an information retrieval system serves as a bridge between the world of authors and world of readers/ users.

FUNCTIONS

While discussing the basic idea of an information retrieval system, we have already seen that it deals with the sources of information on the one hand and the user's requirements on the other hand. The major task is to analyze the contents of the sources of information as well as the user's queries and then to match both to retrieve those items which are relevant. The major functions of an information retrieval system can therefore be:

1. To identify the sources of information relevant to the areas of interest of the target user's community.
2. To analyze the contents of the sources (documents).
3. To represent the contents of the analyzed sources in a way that will be suitable for matching with the user's queries.
4. To analyze user's queries and representation of the query in a form that will be suitable for matching with the database.
5. To make the search statement with the stored database.
6. To retrieve information those are relevant.
7. To make necessary adjustments in the system based on feedback from the users.

DESIGNING OF AN INFORMATION RETRIEVAL SYSTEM

It may be possible for a system to perform perfectly with regard to its stated objectives and functions, but still not be useful. Therefore, if a system is designed carefully, the designers must be aware of the choices which are to be made, and they must consider the consequences of making any choice available to them.

The following factors must be considered explicitly before designing a system:

1. **Objectives :** The overall purpose of the system

2. **Functions :** Major classes of actions or performance required to achieve the objectives.

3. **Performance :** Specific dimensions of required actions, with a requirements statement of the standard or required level of performance for each.

4. **Environment Variables :** Properties of the environment that affect the system and its performance.

Thus, the task involved in the design of an IRS can be divided into four interdependent phases :

1. **Phase I :** deals with basic requirements of the system

2. **Phase II :** deals with the actual design aspects.

3. **Phase ID :** involves the tasks of pilot system installation and its evaluation and required level of performance of required actions.

4. **Phase IV :** Involves the task of implementing the system.

PHASE ONE

This phase actually sets the basic objectives of the system. An effective IRS must have: provision for prompt dissemination of information; provision for filtering of information; provision for right amount of information at the right time; provision for active switching of information; provision for receiving information in the desired form; provision for browsing; provision for getting information in an economic way; provision for current literature; provision for access to other information systems; provision for interpersonal communication and provision for personalized help.

The tasks of the designer may be categorized as here under :

1. To identify the clientele
   (a) those who are now using an existing system
   (b) those who might make use of an improved system
2. To determine the scope of present and potential subject matter interests of the clientele.
3. To determine the permissible expenditures of funds for capital and operating expenses.

1. Identification of Clientele

Clientele may be identified more easily in some cases than in others. If a retrieval system is to be developed for an industrial or governmental organization whose staff members are readily identified, it may be feasible to survey the entire personnel and obtain data on their interest in the use of a new information retrieval activity. However, after a new ISRS system has been developed, it may be expected that the provision of more effective service will attract a larger clientele than the first survey might indicate.

2. Identification of Subject - Matter Interests

A similar approach is suggested when identifying subject - matter interests. Surveys of the clientele will provid some guidance in this regard. However, the clientele will not always be able to predict accurately its own future subject interests, since developments which have not yet been discussed or emphasized in the literature, or which have not yet ever been initiated, may become interesting at a later time. Therefore, the designer, in establishing the capacity of the system, must usually provide for new areas of subject matter as they develop or become important during the life of the system.

There are three types of costs that should be considered viz.,

(a) Capital costs for acquisition and analysis of records and for purchase of a search mechanism.

(b) Operational costs for conducting searches and for provision of services.

(c) Costs involved in not providing suitable information services.

Phase Two

This phase deals with the actual design aspects The system designer has required to take a number of decisions at this stage The major classes of actions or performance required for an IRS to attain its objectives are: Acquisition of source documents; Analysis of source documents; Control of terminology and subject headings; Recording of results of analysis on a searchable medium, Storage of source documents, extracts, abstracts, and/ or bibliographic references; Analysis of questions and development of search strategy; Conducting of search; Delivery of results of search and Utilization of results of search;

(i) Acquisition of Source Documents

Any policy may be established for acquisition. It may be based on : purely arbitrary rules, e.g. acquisition of only those documents that are not regularly accessible through another system of retrieval; subjective decisions, e.g. acquisition of every document that is related to a given subject; acquisition of the total document output of certain publishers or other designated sources.

(ii) Analysis of Source Documents

The analysis of source documents is conducted in the attempt : to infer the intentions of the authors, and to anticipate the interests of the potential readers of documents.

Among the approaches to analysis available are: to use an indexing, classifying or abstracting approach; to provide greater or lesser detail of analysis for any of these approaches; to avoid analysis, as such and instead to use the entire natural language text.

(iii) Control of Terminology and Subject Headings

This "unit operation" of a retrieval system may be considered from three points of view viz., the type of control used; the extent of control; the way in which control is imposed.

The Type of Control Used : The first policy decision to be made, therefore, determines the language that is to be used to record the results of analysis. For example:

By indexing procedures and apparatus, as

- Subject authority lists
- Role indicators or role directors

By classifying procedures and apparatus, as :

- Rigid classification
- Multidimensional classification

Extent of Control of Terminology : The next policy decision determines how rigidly the terminology is to be controlled. Here it is necessary to consider such factors as the number of duplicate entries to be used in an index, what the scope of meaning is for each subject heading of an index, or for each class or sub-class.

Imposition of Control of Terminology : The last decision determines the mechanism to be used to impose terminology control. It is now possible, with modern data processing equipment, to impose control over raw indexing or classifying product of analyst by means of "dictionaries", "thesauri" or indexes which are consulted mechanically or electronically.

(iv) Recording Results of Analysis on Searching Medium

Once a document **has** been acquired and analyzed, and terminological control has been imposed, then it is possible to record on a searching medium the results of the analysis. This may be done on a medium:

(a) Identical with that used to record and / or store the source document (full document, extract);

(b) Separate from that used to record or store the source document.

Example of identical media - marginal - hole punched card systems which have recorded, on the same card, both the analysis and also the source document.

Example of separate media - record index data on some searchable medium together with a serial or accession number referring to the source documents. The source documents are the stored in appropriate order in a separate file, where they may be consulted when the operation of the retrieval system results in their identification by serial number.

(v) Storage of Source Documents

Often, the product of analysis is an abstract, an extract, and / or a bibliographic reference to the document. These products must also be stored in such a way that they can be located readily and used.

Two decisions must be made in this connection :

(a) In what physical form should the source material be stored ?

(b) In what arrangement should the material be stored ?

Physical Form of Storage

In document systems, it is feasible to store a copy of the document with the index only when the unit record either displays the document etc., upon selection, or provides an inexpensive method of printing, enlarging or otherwise delivering a copy of the document. In cases such as these it becomes necessary, from the economic point of view, to keep the amount of such print out (digital computer searching devices) at an absolute minimum. For e.g., a unique document serial number.

Arrangement of Documents

If documents are to be stored in micro film, a number decisions must be made:

(a) Should the arrangement be on unit records or an a continuous record.

(b) If a unit record is used, is it advantageous to attempt to pre-arrange in clusters those documents that have a high likelihood of being of interest ?

(c) If a continuous micro film is used, how long should each roll of film be?

(vi) Analysis of Questions and Development of Search Strategy

The analysis of questions is conducted in order to transform the language of the inquirer into that of the information retrieval system. The search strategy is established in order to exploit in an optimum manner the peculiar capabilities of the retrieval system used.

(vii) Conducting the Search

When a question has been analyzed and a search strategy has been selected, then it is possible to conduct a search. Some of the practical considerations which enter into decisions regarding searching procedures relate to batching of searches or searching questions one at a time, and use of a document versus an aspect system.

(viii) Delivery of the Results of Search

This operation, is dependent on the way in which source documents are stored.If documents are stored separately from index data, then the delivery of search results involves a three step process :

(a) The search produces serial or accession numbers of documents identified.

(b) A file of documents arranged is consulted in order to locate the documents identified during the search.

(c) The documents may then be consulted, withdrawn, or copied.

Thus, we see that in phase two, the designer determines the coverage regarding the subject, the nature of publication, time period, range of users to be covered, range of services to be provided and so on. In fact this phase produces the basic frame work on which the actual tasks of design depends.

Phase Three

This involves the tasks of pilot system installation and its evaluation. It is at this stage, the pilot system is tested not only to determine how does it work but also to identify under what constraints does it work. It is necessary to determine at this level what should be the optimum performance level. The designer should examine various performance requirements to be considered in the planning of an IRS.

Qualitative Requirements : Basically two qualitative requirements are there for an Information Retrieval System, viz.,

(a) ***Subject Coverage*** : This requirement is usually the first to be mentioned while designing a retrieval system. What subject or subjects are to be covered in the system is very important. The determination may be expressed by a delineation of the sources of documents or by the specification of the subjects to be covered, with editorial criteria being laid down at the same time.

(b) ***Precision of Service*** : This requirement may be either qualitative or quantitative in nature. Qualitatively, it involves a specification of the acceptable ratio of pertinent to non pertinent documents that may be supplied in response to a question.

Quantitative Requirements : There are two quantitative requirements, such as

(a) ***Precision of Service*** : Such a specification would involve the limitation of number of documents to be provided in response to a question. Similarly, it might be specified that only the first pertinent response is desired, even if further pertinent responses may be available. Thus, breadth, rather than precision, becomes the operative criterion.

(b) ***Speed*** : An objective of an IRS is to provide service within certain stated time limits. While considering this problem, various factors must be taken into account :

(i) Time for acquisition of records to be incorporated into the system

(ii) Time for analysis and other system input operations.

(iii) Time for analysis of questions and programming of search (by humans or by machines).

(iv) Time for performance of search.

(v) Time for delivery of search results.

(vi) Time for evaluation and use of search results.

Accordingly, there are two factors of speed that warrant consideration in designing a retrieval system : Speed with which unit operations are conducted, acquisition, analysis, recording, storage, search, and delivery must all be considered, as units and as a whole; and Speed with which service is provided (or response time), regardless of the lack of speed involved in other unit operations.

Physical Requirements : The requisite physical requirements may be identified as:

(a) Equipment : When mechanized information retrieval systems are designed, the desired speed of searching (moderated by cost considerations) may dictate the choice of equipment. When such equipment is available, it is often a firm requirement that it be used for the information searching function. The rationale for this decision usually involves consideration of the amortization of equipment costs for 'primary' functions, with the information searching then being asked to bear a part usually only a minor fraction - of the cost of the equipment.

(b) Form and Type of Input : In some organizations, the design of a retrieval system must take into account stringent requirements for form and type of input to the system. If a system will have to depend for analysis of documents on a central processing agency, it is wise to consider searching equipment that will be compatible with the form in which input is provided (eg. Punched cards and magnetic tapes) rather than to stipulate some other medium that would require another step or two in its preparation.

(c) Form and Type of Output : Like input, output must receive due consideration in design of IRS. For example, customer may require a particular size, shape or micro form of output.

(d) Special Conditions : Space limitations and security restrictions are also needed to be taken into consideration.

Space Limitations may lead to a need for miniaturization of documents, they may limit the size of the equipment.

Security Restrictions : Government or business security requirements provide limitations on the accessibility of information which may definitely influence the design of any system designed to supply such information.

(1) Compatibility with other systems : The design of a system may be influences strongly by the need to coordinate with other existing systems or with older systems.

(2) Cost Limitation : Arbitrary limits are often established with regard to the cost of developing and operating a searching system. Decisions must be made often arbitrarily with regard to the optimum allocations of funds among the various unit operations.

(3) Limitation in Personnel Skills : In various areas, system design may call for some minimal amount of training or intelligence on the part of personnel assigned to run the system.

Phase Four

The fourth and final phase involves the task of implementing the system. It is at this stage the pilot system is revised, if necessary, based on the observations from the third phase. Once the final system has been designed, it is installed and is tested in the real life situation. Whenever a new system is designed and installed, it is necessary that the persons who will operate the system are trained adequately. The system designer is probably the right person to propose the best way to train the people. After all these tasks are done, a final report on the system is prepared.

CONCLUSION

Information storage and retrieval systems act as modems between the vast information resources available to humanity and the information seekers at the other end. Their main purpose is to reach the information to the seekers fast and in a reliable manner. Information storage and retrieval systems are catalysers for information utility and its assimilation in the modern society. They help in every human activity in achieving the beneficial societal goals of our civilization.

REFERENCES

1. Chowdhury, G.G. Information Retrieval System. Calcutta : IASLIC, 1994.
2. Kemp, Alister. Knowledge Base Retrieval System. London Aslib, 1988.
3. Kent, A. Information analysis and retrieval. New York: Becker and Heys,1971.
4. Khan, M.T.M. Information Organization and Communication. New Delhi: Ess Ess, 1997.

5. Lancaster, F. Wilfrid. Information Retrieval Systems: Characteristics, testing and evaluation. New York : John Wiley, 1979.

6. Oddy, R.N. [et.al.]. Information Retrieval Research. London : Butterworths,1981.

7. Van Rijsbergen, C.J. Information Retrieval. London : Butterworths, 1979.

8. Vickery, B.C. Techniques of Information Retrieval. London : Butterworths, 1970.

3

Evaluation of Information Retrieval System

Evaluation is a process of feed back against an investment in time, energy, money, knowledge and intelligence. It has measurement from several angles. We evaluate a system in order to ascertain the level of its performance or its value. We can evaluate an information retrieval system from three points of view, namely, how well the system is satisfying its objectives, that is, how well it is satisfying the demands placed upon it; how efficiently it is satisfying its objectives; and finally, whether the system justifies its existence. An evaluation is basically a judgment of worth.

Libraries form an essential part of the chain of human communication. Because knowledge was recorded, individuals formed the repository of knowledge, the bridge between successive generations and between those who generated new information and those required to use it. The amount of information that can be passed on in this way is limited, and socially began to move forward when information of various kinds began to be recorded in relatively permanent forms, which could serve as a substitute for the 'wise-man' in person. Nowadays, the quantity of new information being generated is such that no individual can hope to keep pace with even a small fraction of it, and the problem that we have to face is that endeavouring and ensuring that individuals who need information can obtain it with the minimum of cost and without being overwhelmed by large amounts of irrelevant matter.

PURPOSE OF EVALUATION

Evaluation studies investigate the degree to which the stated goals or expectations have been achieved or the degree to which these can be achieved.

Evaluation studies have the following purposes :

1. To assess a set of goals, a program plan, or a design prior to implementation.
2. To determine whether and how well goals or performance expectations are being fulfilled.
3. To determine specific reasons for successes and failures.
4. To uncover principles underlying a successful program.
5. To explore techniques for increasing program effectiveness.
6. To establish a foundation of further research on the reasons for the relative success of alternative techniques.
7. To improve the means employed for attaining objectives or to redefine sub goals or goals in view of research findings.

EVALUATION CRITERIA

An evaluation study can be conducted from two different points of view ; viz., when it is conducted from managerial point of view, the evaluation study is called management oriented; a study conducted from user's point of view is called user-oriented evaluation study.

User-oriented evaluation should try to answer the following questions :

1. To what extent does the system meet both the expressed and latent needs of its user's community.
2. What are the reasons for the failure of the system to meet the user's needs.
3. What is the cost-effectiveness of the searches made by the users themselves as against those made by the intermediaries.
4. What basic changes are required to improve the output.
5. Can the costs be reduced while maintaining the same level of performance.
6. What would be the possible effect if some new services are introduced or an existing service is erased.

The various parameters of an information retrieval system those are related to each of the evaluation criteria are:-

1. Recall and Precision

The term recall refers to a measure of whether or not a particular item is retrieved or the extent to which the retrieval of wanted items occur. Whenever the user puts his/ her query, it is the responsibility of the system to retrieve all those items which are relevant to the given query. A system may be able to retrieve a proportion of the total relevant documents in response to a given query.

By precision, we mean how precisely does a particular system function. It is quite obvious that while going to retrieve items which are relevant to a given query, the system also retrieves some such documents which are not relevant. These non-relevant items then affect success of the system because the user has to discard all these non relevant items and thus has to waste a significant amount of time the system is able to hold unwanted items in a given situation *is* measured in terms of precision or Precision ratio.

For example: In a given search, the system retrieves 80 items, say out of 60 are relevant and 20 are irrelevant, the precision in this case *is* 75 %.

The general formula for calculation of Recall and precision may be stated as:

Number of Relevant items retrieved

$$\text{Recall} = \frac{\text{Number of Relevant items retrieved}}{\text{Total No. of relevant items in the collection}} \times 100$$

$$\text{Precision} = \frac{\text{Number of Relevant items retrieved}}{\text{Total No. of items retrieved}} \times 100$$

Recall thus relates to the ability of the system to retrieve relevant documents and Precision relates to its ability of not to retrieve non relevant documents. Therefore, ideally the system always attempts to achieve 100% Recall and 100% Precision i.e., it attempts to retrieve all and only the relevant documents. However, it is not possible in actuality, because as we go to increase Recall and Precision tends to decrease. The following example shows the relationship between Recall and Precision of a given search.

Let us suppose that in a given situation, a system retrieves 'a + b' number of documents out of which 'a' number of documents are relevant and 'b' number of documents are left in the collection after conducting the search. This number will be quite large because this represents the whole collection minus the retrieved documents. Out of the 'c + d' number let's say 'c' number of documents are relevant to the query but could not be retrieved and thus have been correctly rejected. Lancaster suggests that these statistics can be represented in a 2 × 2 matrix of the following type, from which the performance figures can easily be determined.

Recall, Precision Matrix

	Relevant	*Non-Relevant*	*Total*
Retrieved	A (Hit)	b (Rejected)	a + b
Non-Retrieved	C (missed)	d (Rejected)	c + d
Total	A + c	b + d	a+b+c+d

In the above table, the system retrieves a number of relevant documents along with 'b' number of non-relevant documents. Using the words of Lancaster, it may be stated that 'a' denotes the 'hit' whereas 'b' denotes the 'noise'. Now out of the remaining 'c + d' number of documents, the system misses 'c' number of documents which should have been retrieved, but it correctly rejects 'd' number of documents which are not relevant to the given query. The Recall and Precision ratio in this case be calculated as:

$$\text{Recall} = \{a / (a + c)\} \times 100$$

$$\text{Precision} = \{a / (a + b)\} \times 100$$

LIMITATION OF RECALL AND PRECISION

The different users may want different levels of recall. A person going to prepare a state-of-the-art report on a topic will like to have all items available on that topic and therefore will go for a high recall. Such a measure is that users very often are unable to specify exactly how many items they want to be retrieved. Recall and Precision depend largely on the relevance of judgments of the user. The judgment is quite subjective and there may be different degree of relevance of the retrieved output.

2. Response : is the average time needed to obtain a response from the system. It depends on following parameters: Organization of stored documents; type of query; location of information center; frequency of receiving of user's queries and size of the collection.

3. User effort : It shows the effort required by the user, which largely depends Upon the following points: Accessibility of the system; availability of guidance of system personnel; volume of retrieved items and facilities for interaction with the system;

4. Form of presentation : It means the forms in which search results are presented to the user. It depends upon: type of display device; nature of output-bibliographic reference, or abstract or full text.

5. Collection coverage : It is the Coverage of the system, that includes type of input device and type and size of storage device; depth of subject analysis, nature of user's demand; nature of core subject area and physical forms of documents.

DESIGN OF EVALUATION PROGRAMME

An evaluation study can be conducted in either of the two environments- laboratory and real. In order to answer the questions unambiguously, an evaluation study must be designed to exclude any extraneous variation which may confuse the results. Laboratory environment is that which controls or eliminates all the variables except those describing certain aspects of the performance of the system that are going to be measured. Real Life is represented by an operational environment.

There are basically two types of evaluation-macro evaluation and micro evaluation.

Macro evaluation is concerned with the level of service product by an information retrieval system. Micro evaluation attempts to discover why does the system perform at a given level and what measures can be taken to improve its level of performance.

STEPS OF EVALUATION

According to F.W. Lancaster there are five major steps involved in the evaluation of Information Retrieval System, which are: Designing the scope of evaluation; Designing the evaluation program; Execution of the evaluation; Analysis and interpretation of results and Modifying the system in the light of the evaluation results. A detailed discussion of the same is given here.

1. Designing the Scope of Evaluation

An evaluation study is usually conducted to determine the level of performance of the given system and also to identify those factors which are the reasons for weaknesses of the system. In other words, an attempt is made to find out the different parameters and their interrelations with a view to assess their contribution towards the overall performance of the system. The first step of an evaluation study entails the preparation of a set of objectives which the given study is going to meet. The purpose and scope of the whole evaluation program is set at this step. It is also considered how the evaluation study will be conducted in a laboratory type set up or in a real life situation, at what level it be evaluated, i.e., macro evaluation or micro evaluation and so on.

2. Designing the Evaluation Programme

This step entails the determination of the parameters on which data are to be collected and also proposes the methodology. A detailed plan of action is to be prepared which is to be followed for collection of data. The detail design of the evaluation program is prepared by supervisory staffs and systems analysts, while the actual evaluation study is executed by other staff members.

3. Execution of the Evaluation

It is needless to mention that this step takes the longest time in an evaluation study. The system personnel collect data in a way prescribed at the design stage. In most cases, repeated number of observations are required to avoid sampling error and biasness. There should be a communication between the evaluator and the designer at this stage so that they can communicate any interesting observation which might call for redesign of the evaluation program.

4. Analysis and Interpretation of Results

The whole fate of the evaluation program rests upon the method of interpretation of results and its accuracy. On the other hand, the evaluator has a set of purpose and objectives of the evaluation program, and on the other the observation i.e. the data collected on different parameters.

Although, the methodology for manipulation of data is determined at the design stage.

Lancaster mentions that the joint use of performance figures and failure analysis should answer most of the questions identified in the work statement for the evaluation.

5. Modifying the System in the Light of the Evaluation Results

Finally, the retrieval system is modified, if necessary, in the light of the result of the evaluation study.

CONCLUSION

It may be concluded that there is still a place for intellectual analysis and that the librarian with his information retrieval techniques still has a significant role to play in the communication of human knowledge. This is certainly true now, only the future will reveal whether it will continue to be so.

REFERENCES

1. Chaudhary, G.G. *Information Retrieval System*. Calcutta: IASLIC, 1994.
2. Khan, M.T.M., *Information Organization and Communication*, New Delhi : Ess Ess, 1977-78.
3. Lancaster, F.W. *Introduction to retrieval system: characteristics, testing and evaluation*. New York: Wiley, 1979.

4

Bibliographic Description And Its Standardization

Bibliographic description is primarily a job comprising taking cognizance element of a documents to describe its identity, content, specification, location, access and dissemination purposes Bibliographic description is the purpose of surrogation of a document A surrogation denotes what a searcher can get by pursuing a document. A bibliographic description is normally used in a document linked operation.

Standardization of the record format is normally prepared bibliographic lists started to be a matter of international concerns from 1960s. International Conference on Cataloguing Principles (ICCP) held in Paris in 1961 set up standards for the headings of authors and title records in catalogues and bibliographies. International Meeting of Cataloguing Experts (IMCE) convened by IFLA in Copenhagen in 1969 was another event of significance in the direction of bibliographic standards.

The first standard in 1974 was meant for description of monographs. It was followed by series of ISBDs for various forms of documents. ISBD (G) lists within its frame all bibliographic elements which are required to describe and identify all types of materials which are likely to appear in library collection. It assigns an order to these elements and prescribed a distinct punctuation system to differentiate them from each other. It consists of eight areas of data elements. These are :

1. Title and statement of responsibility area.
2. Edition area.
3. Material (or type of publication) specific area.
4. Publication distribution etc. area.
5. Physical description area.
6. Series area.
7. Notes area.
8. Standard Numbers.

Many attempts has been taken toward standardization at the international level by means of ISBD, ISBN, ISSN, MARC, UNIMARC, CCF, CDS/ISIS.

ISBN (INTERNATIONAL STANDARD BOOK NUMBER)

In 1967, a system of numbering was developed in Great Britain under the name of Standard Book Number (SBN). Later, it came out in 1971 after it got the approval by the National Standardization Body as (BS4762 : 1971).

BNB started giving the SBN from 1969. In the meantime, with the active participation of a number of countries in this convenient system of book numbering, the SBN has now transferred itself into ISBN.

Formulation

ISBN consists of ten digits representing the four components:

1. Group Identifier (National, Geographical Language or other convenient group)
2. Publisher Identifier
3. Title Identifier

4. Check digit (used for guarding errors in transcription)

Calculation

Example - ISBN 0 85365 306 2

The digits representing the four different components are either hyphenated or separated by space. The check digit is calculated as a modulus of 11 with weights 10 to 2 as shown below taking the previous example :

		Group Identifier	*Publisher Identifier*	*Title Identifier*
1.	The digits of basic no. (9 digits)	0	85365	306
2.	Constant weight for each portion	10	98765	432
3.	Multiply each digit by its weights and add the products	0 +72+40+21+36 +25+12+0+12 = 218		
4.	Divide the sum by modulus 11 to find the remainder	218 ÷ 11 = 19 plus a remainder of 9		
5.	Subtract the remainder from modus 11 to find the check digit	11 – 9 = 2		

So 2 is the check digit, in this case which has been appended to the given ISBN as the last component to make it 10 digit number.

From the above, it is clear that a check digit can be any digit from 0 to 10. When it is 10, it is written as X.

The allocation of publisher identifier digit will have to be controlled and operated by the respective national agencies in each country. The ISO is exactly trying to do this.

ISSN (INTERNATIONAL STANDARD SERIAL NUMBER)

If books can be precisely identified by ISBN, then serials can be easily identified by ISSN. In this area, the publishers and librarians alike had felt the need for something more precise and economical than the title of a serial for quick and easy identification of a serial, especially in the context of mechanized handling of serials data.

Calculation

An ISSN is an eight digit numeric code number to be used for the unique identification of a serial. The last digit is a check digit which is calculated on a modulus of 11 basis using the weightage factor 8 to 2. The check digit is used for trapping transcription errors.

Ex. Indian Journal of Experimental Biology

0019 - 5189

1.	Digit of the base number	0 0 1 9 5 1 8
2.	Weight factors for each position	8 7 6 5 4 3 2
3.	Products of each digit and weighing factor	0 + 0 + 6 + 45 + 20 + 3 + 16 = 90
4.	Divide the sum by modulus 11 to find the remainder	90 ÷ 11 = 8 with remainder of 2
5.	Difference of remainder from modulus 11	11 – 2 = 9

So 9 is the check digit.

The International Centre has been created in Paris which is functioning as the allocation and registration agency for the operation of ISSN.

ISBD (INTERNAL STANDARD BIBLIOGRAPHIC DESCRIPTION)

International Meeting of Cataloguing Experts (IMCE) in Copenhagen in 1969 was set up by the International Working Party to study the possibilities for an ISBD for monographs.

ISBD (M) and ISBD (S) comes out in the year 1974. ISBD (G) published in 1977, other ISBDs are as :

For Cartographic materials	:	1977
For Non Book materials	:	1977
For Antiquarian material	:	1980
For Printed music	:	1980

Rev. Ed. ISBD (S)	:	1977
Rev. Ed. ISBD (M)	:	1978

ISBD (M)

ISBD specified the requirement for the description of printed monographic publications. ISBD (M) has prescribed the following areas of description:

1. Title and Statement of authorship area
2. Edition area
3. Imprint Area
4. Collation Area
5. Series Area
6. Notes Area
7. ISBN, binding and price area.

An "area" is a major section of the bibliographic description comprising data of a particular category or set of categories. An area consists of elements, an element is word or phrase or group of character representing a distinct item of bibliographic information and forming part of an area of the bibliographic description.

ORDER OF ELEMENTS

1. Title and statement of authorship area
   - 1.1 Title Proper
   - 1.2 Parallel Titles, Other Titles and Other Titleing
   - 1.3 Statement of Authority
2. Edition Area
   - 2.1 Edition Statement
   - 2.2 Statement of Authorship relating to the edition
3. Imprint Area
   - 3.1 Place of Publication
   - 3.2 Nature of Publisher
   - 3.3 Date of Publication

3.4 Place of Printing

3.5 Name of Printer

4. Collation Area

4.1 Pagination Area

4.2 Illustration Statement

4.3 Size

4.4 Accompanying Material

5. Series Area

5.1 Series Statement

5.2 Sub Series Statement

5.3 Numbering within series

5.4 ISSN

6. Notes Area

7. ISBN, Binding, Price Area

7.1 ISBN

7.2 Binding *

7.3 Price

* Star and Underlined Statement are optional.

PUNCTUATION

(=) Equal sign precedes a parallel title or a parallel series title

(/) Diagonal slash precedes the first statement of authorship

(&) Ampersand precedes a statement of accompanying material

[ ] Square brackets are used to indicate information taken from sources outside the document

(...) Three dots shows the omission part of an element in certain area

(.-) Full stop space dash space is used to separate each area from the next.

Examples

(1) Theory of classification/ Krishna Kumar - Delhi : Vikas, 1979 . – xii, 51 Op.; 22cm

ISBN 07069 07973 Cloth : Rs. 60

(2) Educational and Social Order/ Bertrand Russel . – Revised and Enlarged ed. – London : George Allen & Unwin, 1975 . – viii, 301p.; 22 cm.

Preview ed. published as: "Education and the modern world."

London: Van Nostrand, 1932.

ISBN 0 486 228769 Paperback : £ 2.00.

ISBD (G)

It provides general framework for the description of documents or library materials. A special feature of this standard is the provision of an area of details, which are special to a particular class of material or type of publication. On the basis of ISBD (G) IFLA has brought out specialized ISBDs dealing with specific types of materials.

The major areas of ISBD (G) are :

Title and statement of responsibility

Edition

Material (or type of publication) specific data

Publication, distribution etc.

Physical description

Series

Notes

Standard Number and terms of availability

The rules for description provided in part 1 of AACR2 are based on the general framework for the description of library materials, the General ISBD, agreed between IFLA and the joint steering committee for revision of AACR. It follows that framework exactly in the order of elements and the prescribed punctuation.

ISBD (G) is intended for use of IFLA working groups in the formulation of other specialist ISBDs and not as a working tool for cataloguers. Besides, it would be used by librarians in the compilation of cataloguing codes.

CONTINUING WORK ON ISBDs

As ISBD Review Committee was formed by IFLA in 1981 to implement a five year review of the ISBDs for monographs, serials, cartographic material and non-book materials, ISBD (M), ISBD (S), ISBD (CM) and ISBD (NBM) with the intention of publishing revisions in 1987. ISBD (PM) - Printed Music was also being reviewed and work proceeded on analytical cataloguing.

The revised edition of ISBD (NBM) came out in 1987. A Manual of Annotated ISBD (M) Examples were compiled by C.P. Ravillions and published by IFLA in 1981 and a Revised edition of International Standard Bibliographic Description for serials, ISBD (S) was published in 1988.

Special attention has also been given to computer files : a Working Group met for the first time in 1986 and the final version of ISBD (CF) was published in 1990. A revised draft of ISBD for rare, antiquarian books, ISBD (A) was circulated for study by appropriate persons in 1998.

Besides the ISBD, there have been two more developments, i.e. ISBN, (International Standard Book Number) and ISSN (International Standard Serial Number). These were developed to identify material by their uniquely given numbers. All these developments have left deep impact on the bibliographic control at global level.

CCF (COMMON COMMUNICATION FORMAT)

International symposium on Bibliographic Exchange Formats in Taormina, Sicily in April 1978 by UNESCO to study the desirability and feasibility of establishing maximum compatibility among the existing bibliographic exchange formats. The symposium was organized by UNISIST, ICSU - AB, IFLA and ISO. These organizations appoints a General Information Programme (PGI) for the design of CCF. The group compared the data elements of other standard formats existing at that time. It was agreed to use the ISO 2709 standard for the structure of the record.

First edition of CCF was published in 1984 and second edition in 1988. In 1990, another publication "Implementation nodes of users of CCF" was issued as a guide.

STRUCTURE OF CCF

The structure of CCF is the implementation of ISO 2709. It consists of:

1. Record Label
2. Directory
3. Data Field
4. Record Separator

1. Record Label

Each CCF records begins with a record label of 24 characters.

0 to 4 - *Record Length* : It includes the length of the label, directory data fields and field separator. A record may have a maximum length of 99999 characters.

5 - *Record Status* : It indicates with a code whether the record is new, replace one, deleted one etc.

6 - Blank

7 - *Bibliographic Level :* It indicates with code e.g. m = monograph, s = serial

8 - Blank

9 - Blank

10 - '2' *The Indicator Length :* Many fields are provided with indicators and indicators requires 2 character position e.g. 01.

11 - '2' the sub field identifier length. Here 2 indicates the two character used as sub field identifier e.g. @A.

12 to 16 - Base address of data. It indicates the location of the first character of the first data field with in a record. It is to be noted that first data fields begins after the last directory in a record.

17 to 19 - Blank

20 - '4' The length of a *"length of data field"*. Here 4 indicates that a data field of four character length. Hence, the maximum length of data field can be of 9999 characters.

21 - '5' The length of starting character position in the directory. Here '5' indicates that starting character position is represented by 5 digits.

22 - '2' The length of implementation defined - selection of each entry in the directory of the two characters indicated in this position by *'2'*, one character indicates the segment identifier, and the other the occurrence identifier.

2. Directory

Directory is of 14 character length and comprises of 5 parts. They are:

1. Tag
2. Length of data field
3. Starting Character Position
4. Segment Identifier
5. Occurrence Identifier

Tag

It is a three character numeric code representing the data field which corresponds to the directory entry. E.g. 020.

Length of Data field

It indicates the length of a data field with 4 digits e.g. 0048. The length of the data field includes the length of indicators, sub field identifiers, data and field separator, all in terms of characters.

Starting Character Position

It is a five digit number indicating the position of the first character of a data field counted from the base address of data.

Segment Identifier

It is a single character chosen from numerals (0 to 9) and / or capital letters (A to Z) it is used to differentiate multiple occurrences of data fields within the same record segment.

Ex.	50000260 031802
500	indicates tag number
0026	indicates the length of data field.
00318	indicates starting character position
0	indicates the first segment
2	indicates the third occurrence.

3. Data Fields

There are a four basic components of a data field. They are:

1. Indicators
2. Sub field Identifier
3. Sub field
4. Field Separator

More than one sub field may be accommodated within the same data field. Every sub field is preceded by a sub field identifier.

Indicators

Indicators are of 2 digits of which convey a distinct meaning.

Sub Field Identifier

It consists of two character of which one is @ and the other one is a capital letter (A to Z).

Sub Field

It contains the data element. A sub field is followed by either another sub field identifier or a data field separator.

Data Field Separator

It is the last character of a data field

Ex. 11@ A Tagore @ BR.N / @ D1861-1941 @E 070 •

1 (1st Character)	Indicates that the person has primary responsibility for the contents of the items described in this segment of record.
1 (2nd Character)	the form of the name of the person comes from the authority file of the agency.
@A	The first sub field identifier
Tagore	The data element of the first sub field, which is the surname of the person
@B	The second sub field identifier.
R.N	The data element of the second sub field which are the initials of the forename of the author.
@ D	The third sub field identifier.
1861-1941	Data element of the third sub field.
@E	The fourth sub field identifier. It shows that the person's role in that of the author.
070	Data element of the fourth sub field
•	Data field separator.

4. Record Separator

The last data field separator is followed by the record separator which is the final character of the record.

Some Tag Number of CCF List of Data Elements

Tag	*Name*
001	Record Identifier
015	Bibliographic level of sec. Segment
020	Source of Record
022	Date Entered on File
031	Language and Script of Record
040	Language and Script of Item
060	Type of Material
100	ISBN
101	ISSN
102	CODED
110	National bibliography number
200	Title
210	Parallel Title
260	Edition Statement
300	Name of Person
400	Place of Publication
440	Date of Publication
460	Physical Description
490	Part Statement (Say Vol. Pages)
500	Note
610	Classification Scheme Notation
620	Subject Description

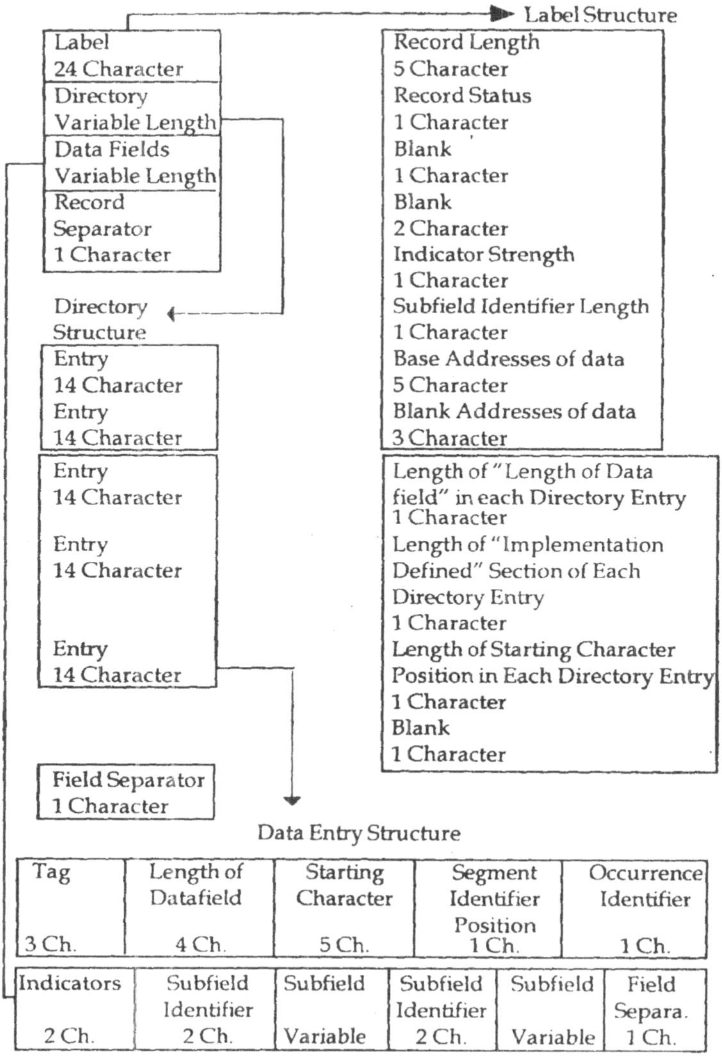

Diagrammatic Representation of the CCF Record Structure

CDS/ISIS (COMPUTERIZED DOCUMENTATION SERVICE/ INTEGRATED SET OF INFORMATION SYSTEM)

CDS/ISIS has promoted standardization of bibliographical record format at international level and has made exchange and transfer of information between libraries and research institutions easier CDS/ ISIS designed and developed by UNESCO from time to time and made it first available in 1985. Different versions of this package is given below

2.3 ver 1989

2.32 ver 1990

3.0 ver 1992

3.07 ver 1993

3.071 ver 1995

Version 3.071 with full LAN support and also for various platform like DOS, NOVEL network, VAX / VMS. The windows version of CDS/ ISIS is in beta phase and is presently available only on the internet.

This is a menu driven package, Worldwide use of CDS/ ISIS for database creation, follows the standards of ISO 2709 for describing the bibliographical records. We can define database according to our own convenience and follows the AACR-II rules.

Standardization of the bibliographic records can easily be understood with defining database, by this package. Database is defined in four steps:

I	Step	To define field description table
II	Step	To define display format
III	Step	To define field select table
IV	Step	To define worksheet

I. Step - Field Definition Table

The first step in database creation is to fill FDT in which we have to define the fields The screen will show the following:

Field Definition Table			*FDT Database*		
Tag	Name	Len	Type	Rep.	Delimiters
300	Author	50	X	R	abc
200	Title	250	X	R	
400	Imprint	100	X	R	abc

The meaning of the columns are given below :

Tag : Tag is a numeric identifier for the field. In CDS/ISIS, Tag no. of CCF is used because it is used universally for database.

Name : Name help us to identify the field (ex. Author, title, member).

Len : Len is a length of the field. We have to give an appropriate no. of letters, the field may contain as length.

Type : Field type can be accepted as X for alphanumeric nature of the field. If the field is only alphabetical, it will be A and if the field *is* in numeric contents, then N is used

Rep. : It defines whether the field is repeatable or **not.** If repeatable, R is represented, if not, left it blank.

Delimiters : Delimiters means the letter used for dividing fields. Eg. abc. It is given without space and any punctuation marks. It generally defines that the field must be separated in three different sub fields.

Ex. Writer's name - can be divided into two parts —

	Surname	Forename
Two delimiters	a	b

Given as a b -

II. Step - Display Format

Display format decides the way in which records will appear on the screen when we record information. It is used for printing output also. Fields can be specified by using variable in part of tag. Thus, V10 means display the contents of the field 10.

Ex.

954

J64D Nehru, Jawahar Lal

Discovery of India Bombay

Education Press, 1952

56821 XV, 268 p. (Indian Heritage Series)

Key words: History - India; History; India

Display format

#, V610 / C12, v300^b, V300^a/ C12, V200

X4, V400A/ C (10,12) V400B V440/ V120, C12,

V490, X4, V480/ C12 "Keywords" #

We can fill the format according to standard cataloguing rules say AACRII.

III. Step - Field Select Table

CDS/ISIS automatically prepares an index and is called inverted file. The extraction of terms that are to go to the index file is controlled by FST.

Database name		*FST for Inverted File*
ID	IT	Data Extraction format
300	1	Mhl, V300^b, V300^a
200	0	Mhl,V200
610	0	Mhl, V610

IT Indexing Technique

0 is used when whole field is to be indexed:

1 when subfield indexed

2 when word is taken into triangular brackets

3 when the words will be taken between slash

4 when the each word of the field is indexed.

Data Extraction Format

We have to state the field in the record form where the terms should come. Fields should be specified with v in front of the tags.

IV. Step - Worksheet

Worksheet is meant for entering data into the database. Nineteen fields is the limit for one page. The program for defining worksheet will be taken into eight prompts for each field.

1. Enter field tag
2. Enter L/C position of the field name
3. Edit Replace
4. Enter L/ C position of field value
5. Attribute
6. Length, as default value as in the FDT
7. Help message
8. Enter Default Value

After defining all the four steps, database is to start for inputting data.

MARC (MACHINE READABLE CATALOGUE) RECORD FORMAT

MARC commenced as a pilot project in 1966 in Library of Congress. In the year 1967, a revised MARC - II was developed. MARC follows AACRII.

MARC format is developed for the purpose of communicating bibliographic information to a large number of libraries.

The MARC record involves four elements:

1. The Leader or Record Label
2. The Directory
3. Control Field
4. Variable Data Field.

The MARC format contains specification for encoding data elements needed to describe, retrieve and control various types of bibliographic material. This format is extended to books, series, cartographic materials, Music and A-V materials.

Leader	Directory	Control Fields	Variable Data Field

1. Leader or Record Label

It is a fixed field of 24 characters. They are used to indicate nine types of data such as length, status type and bibliographic level of the record and blank character, sub field Code, base address etc

1-5	Record length indicates total number of characters used in the records
6	Record status tells whether it is new (n), changed (c) or deleted record (d)
7-10	Implementation Code
	7 Type of Record means whether printed or not
	8 Class of record means bibliographic level whether it is analytic (a), monograph (m), serial (s) or collection (c) 9-10 Blanks
11	Indicator Count
12	Sub field mark count
13-17	Base address of data
18	Encoding level
19-20	Blanks
21-24	Directory Map
21	Length of data field
22	Length of starting character portion
23-24	Blank

Ex.

01543	n	a	m	f6	2	2	00205	F	Ff	4	5	ff
1-5	6	7	8	9-10	11	12	13-17	18	19-20	21	22	23-24

2. Directory

It is an index to the location of the variable field within a record. It is made up of series of fixed length fields consisting of tags and the starting character position field. The directory begins immediately after the leader and end always with a field terminator. The number of entries in the directory depends on the number of variable data fields in the record.

Element no.		*No. of Character*	*Character Position in the directory*
1	Tag	3	0-2
2	Field Length	4	3-6
3	Starting Character Position	5	7-11

Tag is a 3 character number which identifies the field.

Field length is the no. of characters in the field identified by the tag

Starting Character Position : 4 character number which identifies the position of the field in the record of the first character of a field relative to the base address of data.

e.g. 0039 - the first character of the first field following the directory is numbered as 0.

3. Control Fields

Directory is followed by the control fields which are data fields consisting of information such LC card no., date of entry in the file, date of publication, language of text, country of publisher etc. Fields 001 - 009 are defined as control fields. Control fields have no indicators and no-sub field.

Record Directory

Field-I			*Field-II*			...		*Field-N*			
Tag	Length	Starting Character Position	Tag	Length	Starting Character Position		Tag	Length	Starting Character Position	F/T	

Control Fields

Data Element-1	Data Element-2	Data Element-3	.....	Data Element-n	F/T

Variable Fields

Variable Field-1 Variable Field-2

Indicator	Subfield Code	Data Element	Subfield Code	Data Element	....	Subfield Code	Data Element	F/T	Indicator	Subfield Code	Data Element	...	Subfield Code	Data Element	F/T	...	F/T	R/T

F/T = Field Indicator R/T = Record Terminator

Figure shows a sample of the Library of Congress Card in the MARC format.

0046 1	n	a	m	b b	2	2	0018 1	bab450 0	00100130000 0	00800410001 3	02000150005 4

039001800069	050002200087	082001500109	100002300124	245009900147

26000400246	300002500280	504004100305	650001600346	650001800362

LC Card Number Fixed Length Data Elements

ƀƀƀ	86	073221	ƀ	F	870311	s	1987	ƀƀƀƀ	nyu	ƀƀƀƀ	ƀ	ƀ	Bƀƀƀƀ00010ƀ	eng	ƀ	ƀ	f

ISBN			Level of Cat Detail			LC Call Number		
ƀƀ	≠a0824507851	F	0ƀ	≠a2≠b3≠c3≠d3≠c3	F	0ƀ	≠aBV4813≠ƀ. F73ƀ1987	F

Dewey Number		Main Entry			Title	
ƀƀ	≠a248. 3'4≠219	b	10	≠aFreeman. bLaurence	F	10	≠aLightbwithiinb≠btheb

Innerƀpathƀofbmeditationƀ	≠cLaurenceƀFreemanƀ:forewodbbyYehudibMenuthin	F

Imprint			Collation		
0ƀ	≠aNewƀYork;≠ƀCrossroad≠c 1987	F	ƀƀ	≠axi.ƀ115ƀpƀ;≠c22ƀcm	F

Note

ƀƀ	≠aIncludesƀbibliographicalƀreferences	F

Subject Headings

ƀ0	≠aMeditation	F	ƀ0	≠aContemplation	R

ƀ — Blank F — Field terminator R — End of Record ≠ — delimiter

Frerman, Laurence.

Light within: the inner path of meditation/Laurence Freeman; Foreword by Yahudi Menuhin — New York: Crossroad, 1987.

xi, 115p;22cm.

Includes bibliographical references.

ISBN 0-8245-0785-1

1. Meditation 2. Contemplation 1. Title

NV4813.F73 1987 248.3'4–dc19 86–73221

AACR2MARC

Library of Congress

4. Variable Data Fields

Variable data fields are made up of single as well as groups of data elements. Each variable data field consists of indicators, sub field codes, identified the constituent data element of a variable field.

UNIMARC

In 1977, the IFLA International Office for UBC published UNIMARC. In 1980, 2nd edition came with specification for cartographic material. UNIMARC developed as a international interchange of bibliographic data. It is a communication format which would be necessitate the writing and maintaining of only two conversion programs - one from national format to the UNIMARC and the other from the UNIMARC to the national format.

STRUCTURE OF UNIMARC

Its structure contains:

1. Record Label
2. Directory
3. Variable Control Fields
4. Variable Data Fields

1. Record Label

It is of 24 characters:

Data Elements	*No of Characters*
Record Length	5
Record Status	1
Implementation Code	4
Indicator Length	1
Sub field Identifier	1
Base Address of data	5
Add. Record Definition	3
Directory Map	3
F/T	1

Example

00798	n	a m 1	b	2	2	00145	1 b b	450 b

2. Directory

It is an index to the variable field within a record.

Data Elements	*No.of Characters*
lag	3
Length of Data field	4
Starting character position	5

Example

Tag	LDF	SCP
200	0056	00298

3. Variable Control Field

Directory is followed by the control field.

Example

Data	F/T

4. Variable Data Field

Variable data fields are groups of data elements.

Data Elements	*No.of Characters*
Indicators	2
Sub field Identifier	2
Data	Variable
Field Terminator	1

Example

B1	$a Kumar	$b Narendra	F/T

UNIMARC uses a special block structure in place of areas:

Type of Data	*Blocks*	*Fields*
Identifiers (Item and Record)	Block 0	0nn Fields
Coded Information	Block 1	1nn Fields
Descriptive Paragraph Notes	Block 2 Block 3	2nn Fields 3nn Fields
Link to other works	Block 4	4nn Fields
Variant Titles	Block 5	5nn Fields
Subject Analysis	Block 6	6nn Fields
Intellectual Responsibilities	Block 7	7nn Fields

ISBD data is specially accommodated in Block 2 i.e. descriptive paragraph.

UNINARC is maintained by IFLA, UBCIM Office. Reviews and adjustments are made every 3-4 years. UNIMARC based data is now supported in several systems such as MINISIS and CDS/ISIS.

UNISIST REFERENCE MANUAL

Reference Manual was the effort of UNESCO in 1974 The second edition was brought out in 1981. The manual was intended to be a CCF. This manual was the combined effort of working group made up by ISO, FID, IFLA, IMS, OECD members. It attempted to define a minimum set of data elements which could be agreed upon by abstracting and Indexing services for interchange records. The user of Reference Manual were Indexing and Abstracting agencies.

Indian Standard

Bureau of Indian Standards had evolved a standard for bibliographic references in 1963 for use in non-computerized systems. The sixteenth Indian Standards Convention of ISI held in Bhopal in October 1975 discussed the issue of standardization of bibliographic information in the context of machine readable records and publication of standard (IS: 11370 - 1985) titled "Guide for data elements and record format for computer based bibliographic description of different kinds of documents in 1986".

Structure of this format conform to ISO - 2709 - 1981

Among the data elements descriptive block is based on ISBD. Subject analysis block includes POPSI, PRECIS.

CONCLUSION

From the above description, We may conclude that it is clear that many efforts were taken in developing the machine readable format at the international level. Different organizations involved in such type of efforts still working in the same light to develop such a fool proof common communication format which will satisfy the present and future needs with the exploration of information at the international level. So it must be the combined effort of all the nations who lie to share the bibliographic records and tends the world to develop in more effective way.

REFERENCES

1. Guha B, *Documentation and Information. Calcutta, World Press, 1983.*
2. Khan, M.T.M., *Information Organization and Communication. New Delhi; Ess Ess, 1998.*
3. Girija Kumar and Krishan Kumar, *Theory of Cataloguing. 5th ed., New Delhi Vikas, 2000.*
4. Ravichandra Rao, I.K., *Library Automation.*
5. Satyanarayana, N R., *Manual of Computerization in Libraries. New Delhi, Vishwa, 1995.*

6. Sharma, U.C., Rawtani, M.R., *Librarianship Today and Tomorrow. New Delhi, Ess, 1997.*

7. Tedd, Lucy *A., An introduction to Computer Based Library System. 2nd edition,Chichester, John Wiley, 1984.*

Part III
Indexing

5

Developments in Subject Indexing

Indexing is an important aspect of a document retrieval. Subject indexing attempts to indicate the subject contents of a document to a searcher of a bibliographic catalogue or a database.

The need for providing subject approach to the document made the determining of an appropriate subject heading a necessity in cataloging as well as in indexing. Most of the documents, however, deal with composite subjects consisting of a number of components.

SUBJECT INDEXING TECHNIQUES

The indexing technique owes its origin to the traditional book index. From time to time, the book indexes were made more and more specific. Specific aspects of a topic or subject were indicate in the form of subject heading and location of each in the text was Indicated. The book index and its continuous refinements has had its effects on the indexing technique which were introduced and nurtured by Cutter, Kaiser, Coates, Ranganthan and others.

PROBLEMS INVOLVED IN SUBJECT INDEXING

Compilation of a book index is quite easy. But the

construction of a bibliographical or subject index is not so easy. Finding out the correct subject of a document and specifying it in indexing language so that there is no problem of synonyms and homonyms, etc., and the subject is retrieved quickly on demand is rather a very complex job. The indexing language is used to represent the subject contents so that a searchable file is constructed for easy and quick retrieval. It is a rare phenomenon that a specific document is represent by a single term. Normally most of the documents these days deal with compound and complex subjects comprising of a number of concepts. These subject can be represented by a more than one term only. When a subject consists of a number of components, the ordering or sequencing of the components brings in many problems. These components can be arranged in six ways, four in twenty four ways and five in 120 ways and so on. But out of these arrangements which one is the most appropriate or useful to the users is not easy to determine. The contributions of Cutter, Kaiser, Coates, Ranganathan, Farradane and Sharp towards subject indexing trace the evolution of indexing techniques.

CUTTER'S CONTRIBUTION

Subject cataloguing has influenced indexing techniques. Cutter was the first to discuss the concept of specific subject in his "Rules for Dictionary Catalogue" in 1876. He advocated the entry of a work under its specific subject heading and not under the subject heading of the class which includes that subject. Cutter also gave the rules of entry for multiword headings. He suggested entering "a compound subject name by its first word, inverting the phrase only where some other word is decidedly more significant or is often used alone with the same meaning as the whole name." Cutter, however, did not specify as how to find out which one of the component parts of a multiword compound heading would be decidedly more significant. To find this out, the indexer was to rely on his own judgement or flair.

KAISER'S CONTRIBUTION

In 1911, J. Kaiser in his systematic indexing laid down a theoretical basis for fixing the order of significance among various components of a composite heading. He recommended that a subject should be analysed to divide the constituent concepts into two categories - Concrete and Process. He categorized things, places and abstract terms not signifying action as concretes and the term signifying action as processes. For instance, if the subject of a document is the classification of books, then the books are Concrete and classification Process. The order of components advocated by Kaiser was Concrete and Process, or Concrete was to be the entry word. Locality-topic combination, however, were to have double entry. 'Export of Wheat' subject shall have WHEAT–EXPORT as the subject heading. But 'Export of Wheat from India' shall have the following two subject - headings:

WHEAT - INDIA - EXPORT

INDIA - WHEAT - EXPORT

Thus by fixing the order of significance of the components of a compound subject, Kaiser endeavoured to resolve the uncertainty which Cutter had left untouched.

STANDARD LISTS OF SUBJECT HEADINGS

The indexer in his own way cannot practice subject indexing as the entries in a subject index are made in accordance with specific rules governing their choice, style and terminology. If compiled otherwise, the subject index is bound to have many variations in subject headings, which in turn render it less useful to the user.

To derive a subject heading, one method is to make use of a printed list of subject headings. Following are some of the important lists of subject headings :

1. Sears List of Subject Headings (1923)
2. Library of Congress List of Subject Headings (1971)
3. Medical Subject Headings (1950s)

These lists aim to provide one form of subject headings under which all documents on a given subject can be listed.

1. Sears Lists of Subject Headings

Sears List was first published in 1923. It had then a collection of such subject headings as could be useful for small libraries. Later on, its scope was enlarged so as to make it equally useful for medium size libraries. This lists consists of pre-coordinate indexing vocabulary and is based on the principle of specificity. The subject heading to be used is written in bold type. Each subject heading is followed by headings by x or xx. These can respectively be used to prepare see and see also references.

Example: Libraries, College and University

x College libraries; Libraries, University; University Libraries

xx Colleges and universities. College libraries

See

Libraries, College and University

Libraries, University

See

Libraries, College and University

Colleges and University

See also

Libraries, College and University

The Sears List recommends the principle of specific entry. The 'most specific term' to be used for preparing a subject entry is the 'subject heading' which accurately and precisely represents the contents of the document. The list prefers the use of popular or common names over the scientific or technical names. Out of several synonyms, the list has decided in favour of one and uses it consistently. Mostly, the list provides direct headings; in some cases, however, inverted headings have also been used. Detailed sub-divisions for some subjects have been provided, and indexers are permitted to construct the similar sub-divisions for other headings of the same type. Necessary direction have also been provided.

2. LC List of Subject Headings

Though LC Subject Headings started appearing earlier, the first edition of LC list appeared in 1911. The LC list follows the principles of Cutter and reflects the practices of the Library of Congress. Only those subject headings have been included in the LC list which were chosen for the dictionary catalogue of the Library of Congress.

LC list is more comprehensive and suits larger collections.

Symbol 'sa' indicates 'see also'; 'x' means make 'see' reference from; and 'xx' indicates that 'see also' reference be made from the heading preceded by it. The words (direct) and (indirect) indicate those heading which are subdivided by place, indirectly or directly.

The LC list suits the American Libraries the best. For other countries, it remains inadequate. All the marks of punctuation in the LC list are ambiguous and have no particular meaning. The LC list should utilize subject headings drawn from the literature and fit them into prescribed grammatical patterns. The LC list is thus, the most comprehensive list of subject headings in the English language.

3. Medical Subject Headings

Besides the general lists of subject heading, a number of special lists to cater to the special requirements have been developed. Most of them follow the same pattern as of LC list, but they provide greater specificity and detailed sib-divisions. The list of medical subject headings is a typical example of such lists. This list is published as Part 2 of the Index Medicus since the subject headings are not pre-coordinated, one may have to endure a fair amount of sequential scanning in the search for information on a specific composite subject. A detailed network of references has been provided but different symbols have been used. A non preferred term lead to more than one preferred term. The notation in the parenthesis following each heading indicates the subject categories where it will be found in the second part of the list.

COATES' CONTRIBUTION

E.J. Coates' contribution towards subject indexing is very significant. His order of significance among various components of a compound subject is Thing, Material and Action. According to Coates, 'the most significant term in a compound subject is the one which is most readily available to the memory of the enquirers' or 'the enquirer's choice... will fall on that word, which gives the most definite image". In a concept, "springing cat", the image of cat comes to our mind first and then only we think of the act springing. And without 'cat', the idea of 'springing' can not be visualized. The order of the component terms in a compound subject heading will have to be the same as our thinking process.

RANGANATHAN'S CONTRIBUTION

Early efforts to arrive at a suitable subject heading were to some extent ad hoc solution without any sound theoretical base. The clear understanding of the concept of specific subject and the vision to formulate it on scientific basis could only offer right solutions to the problem.

Ranganathan did it through his chain indexing. It uses a classificatory base, and the indexer takes over from where the classifier leaves. The components of a compound subject in chain indexing get automatically arranged in the order of Time, Space, Energy, Matter and Personality; or Personality, Matter, Energy, Space and Time.

FARRADANE'S CONTRIBUTION

The sequence of components in a subject formulation was all important before J.E.L. Farradane who has provided a new approach which is based on the relationship that exists between each pair of components. He recognizes nine types of relationships, such as association, comparison, concurrence, dimensional, distinctness, equivalence etc. These relationships are indicated by various operators or symbols. A relevant operator is inserted between two components to show their correct relationship. Operator ';' indicates 'association'. The subject formulation for the document. "Disease of Eyes" shall be Eyes/ ; Diseases. Similarly, the subject formulation for a documents "Treatment of the Diseases of Eyes" shall be Eyes/; Diseases/ - Treatment. Operator '-' represents 'Action' relationship here. This subject formulation can also be represented in the following order of components :

Treatment-/ Diseases; / Eyes.

Both the components and operators have been reversed. By changing the direction of the operators, the same relationship can be retained between the pair of terms. This naturally lessens the importance of sequence order of significance of terms in a subject formulation.

SHARP'S CONTRIBUTION

In conventional indexing, access is provided from each of the component terms by rotation or cycling so as to have a network of references. It is done to ensure maximum access. Against this, Sharp is of the view that specific subject formulations, having all the components, may not be of much use to the seekers of information. He believes that most of the users are able to cite more than one, but not all the components constituting a specific subject. Also the users do not get correct answers because the combination of components they are searching for are not there. Sharp in his SLIC (Selective Listing In Combination) indexing system ensures optimum economy in the bulk of index by providing combinations irrespective of the citation order. Sharp finds out only some selective combinations of components constituting the subject of the document for using as index headings. Those combinations which form the beginning of larger combinations are excluded and this reduces the bulk of an index.

AUSTIN'S CONTRIBUTION

PRECIS – the PREserved Context Index System- was developed by Dereck Austin in the later part of 1960s as an alternative procedure for deriving subject heading and index entries for British National Bibliography (BNB) which since 1952, for about 20 years was following Chain Indexing for deriving subject index entries. Two most important factors played significant role in looking for an alternative method which ultimately resulted in the development of PRECIS:

- Idea of replacing chain indexing technique of BNB.
- The decision of the British library to generate computer produced BNB with all the indexes.

BHARTACHARYYA'S CONTRIBUTION

In historical context, chain indexing has been a significant landmark which received its due recognition both at home and abroad. The inherent weakness of chain indexing has been its dependence on a scheme of classification. Another weakness of chain indexing was its disappearing chain. In view of this situation the information scientists G.Bhattacharyya and A.Neelameghan at the DRTC, Bangalore directed themselves to the task of developing an indexing system free from these limitations. The POstulate based Permuted Subject Indexing (POPSI) is the result of these efforts. POPSI came to be developed almost at the same time when Derek Austin was developing PRECIS in England.

CRAVEN'S CONTRIBUTION

Timothy C. Craven has developed the Nested Phrase Indexing System (NEPHIS). As in the case of Preserved Context Indexing System, an input string of indexing terms is constructed in this. The complete input string is co-extensive with the subject of the document to be indexed, various parts of the string are permuted by a computer to cater for different access points in that string. The input string in this indexing system takes the basic form of a noun phrase into which other phrases are nested. Four special characters –<, >, ? and @– when inserted into the string, make the computer to show a particular part of the input string as access point and to display the rest of string otherwise for context purpose. Though NEPHIS is easy to learn and use, yet it lacks the versatility of PRECIS and POPSI. For smaller collections, it is all right.

INDEXING LANGUAGE

The problems of natural language make it necessary to have a separate language for indexing which has "power to control vocabulary flexibility to show relation of different concepts and facility to build up a searchable file, providing access to all possible access points of users". This is the indexing language. An indexing language is thus an artificial language which is adapted to the requirements of indexing.

Once information is ascertained, it is to be recorded in some (terms or group of terms) for easy identification, i.e., indexing language. Indexing language is of two types - Derived Term Type and Assigned Term Type.

In the derived term system, all index terms are taken from the document itself. In the assigned term system, it is the indexer who constructs the index terms or descriptors. The latter is an intellectual method involving the finding out of specific subject of the document and assigning an appropriate subject heading. Thus, author indexes, title indexes, citation indexes and natural language indexes are derived term systems, whereas all indexing language with vocabulary control devices, such as thesauri, subject heading list etc. are assigned term systems. A lack of structuring, logic or sense in indexing will produce irrelevant output or what is popularly known as 'garbage in garbage out'.

NATURAL LANGUAGE

Natural language has some advantages. Its vocabulary is up-to-date and it keeps on growing assimilating new concepts as soon as they come into being. It has its syntax and rules of grammar which make it to convey correct meaning of a specific subject. These advantages not with standing natural language is not helpful in organizing an index file which is a must for information retrieval. Then natural language suffers from the problems of homonyms and synonyms because of its flexibility.

ARTIFICIAL LANGUAGE

The list of subject headings, classification schemes and thesauri are representatives of indexing languages. Because of controlled vocabulary of indexing language, it is exact and precise. And there is no problem of synonyms and homonyms because 'see' and 'see also' references as also 'use' references take care of these. The micro-documents of these days require a number of components to specify their subject contents. The sequencing of these components is done according to the rules of syntax of particular indexing techniques. For instance, the chain procedure, PRECIS, POPSI etc. have their own rules of syntax for the formulation of subject representation of a document.

ROTATION OF COMPONENT TERMS

When a subject has been formulated in the preferred index language, it provides only a single access in the index file. For providing access from the other component terms, indexing language has provided a mechanism of rotation of component terms. This rotation brings each of the component terms as a lead term by turn. Since these lead terms are used in association with other component terms, the context in every case remains intact. It has only one specific subject entry, rest of them represent broader subjects. A good indexing system, however is that which rotates the components terms and at the same time keeps the context of the entry term intact with other component terms.

SYNDETIC DEVICES

Indexing language being an artificial language needs some guidance for the users for its proper use. This is done with the help of syndetic devices which include 'see' and 'see also' references, 'use' or 'UF' symbols, scope, notes, glosses, inverted headings, etc. 'See' references direct the user from the synonyms to the term which has been in the index: example

DRTC see Documentation Research and Training Centre.

Simla see Shimla

In a thesaurus, the job of 'see' reference is performed by 'use' reference and the users are guided to the preferred index term. Also the users aredirected from the preferred term to all the rejected terms with help of 'UF' symbol.

FROGS

UF Rana UF Toads

Related index terms scattered throughout the index are linked with the help of 'see also' references. These references link either coordinate or collateral terms or connect general with specific headings.

Disabled

See also Blinds; Clipped; Deaf; Sick.

In some thesauri, glosses in the form of notes and explanations are added to the index terms so that these are understood and used correctly. Similarly, scope notes 'SN' are in other thesauri for the same purpose. Example:

Acceleration

SN The process of progressing through the school grades at a rate faster then that of the average child.

In order to bring related entries together, inversion of index terms is resorted to with the help of a comma, Example-

Randhawa, Mohinder Singh

Documentation, Definition of

Various syndetic devices make the artificial indexing language more meaningful and workable. They also bring organic unity in the index file.

Thus, we can say that an index is an important tool, which helps in retrieval of information on a particular subject. The improvement of index operational tool has been a continuous process. So different people from time to time have contributed in the development of subject indexing.

REFERENCES

1. Bhattacharya, G. and Neelameghan, A. *Postulate based subject heading for dictionary catalogue system. New Delhi: DRTC, 1969.*
2. Foskett, A.C. *The subject approach to information. London: Clive Bingley, 1970.*
3. Ghosh, S.B. and Satpathi, J.N. *Subject Indexing Systems: Concepts, methods and Techniques. Calcutta: Indian Association of Special Libraries and Information Centres, 1998.*
4. Guha, B, *Documentation and information services: techniques and systems. Calcutta: World, 1983.*
5. Parasher, R.G. *information and its communication. New Delhi: Medallion, 1991.*
6. Ranganathan, S.R. *Subject heading and fact analysis. Journal of Documentation 20; 1954.*

6

Indexing and Its Steps

The principle function of any library is to make the information it contains available to the library users at their request. In order to fulfill this function, the information, which is stored in the library, must be recovered, i.e., retrieved, from the store. The process of recovering or retrieving information is called Information Retrieval. Indexing is one of the activities that support the process of information retrieval.

The process of indexing involves a selection of words or ideas from a graphic record on the basis of well-defined rules. The purpose of indexing is to facilitate the identification or selection of desired documents after they have been sorted and shelved or stored.

DEFINITION

J. Rothman in Encyclopaedia of Library & Information Science clearly defines index as a device that serves as a pointer or indicator, most often an alphabetic list that includes subjects and names of people or places that are considered to be of special significance in a graphical record. According to G.S.Bonn an index is a detailed alphabetical list of names, terms, topics, places, formulas, numbers or other significant terms in a completed work with exact page references to material discussed in this work. Thus an index is "a systematically arranged list giving enough information about each item to enable it to be identified and traced."

INDEXING

Indexing is not only a process of making the entries of an index, it is something related to the organization of the entries in a file in a pre-determined order and supplementing the entries with all sorts of cross-references that is, organizing a searchable file, is the sole purpose of the indexing.

The analytical process of indexing involves identifying and selecting words, descriptors or index terms or ideas from a graphical record on the basis of predetermined and well-defined rules. This process of identification, selection and assignment identifiers labels etc., facilitate retrieval of specific documents or information. The pertinent document from millions of micro-documents is identified by appropriate symbolism and the most commonly used symbols may be, words, terms, molecular formulas - chemical, compounds, biological organisms, patents etc.

As the indexing style grows in inwardness, the process becomes sophisticated i.e., the indexer has to make synthetic and syndatic approach. While scanning the documents for indexing, efforts are made to include all possible approach points of users and exclude all possibilities that the users may consider trivials. Identifiers are interlinked which facilitates search of the users. In this process of indexing essential operations are - scanning the documents, analyzing the contents of the documents according to pre-determined criteria, tagging individual items with appropriate identifiers and adding locative information to each identifier for the indication of its location in the store.

PURPOSE

Indexing has the following purposes.

1. Indexes in general guide users to documents and other things, and they are not, however, the material itself. Index entries are not intended to describe the material indexed.
2. Author indexes guide users to names of people and lead searches to documents related by subject, because authors tend to specialise. There are many kinds of specialised indexes such as indexes to molecular formulae, organic rings, taxonomic names and citations.
3. Indexes provide guide to material that the user may wish to recall or that he may know exists; that is indexes are used for questions of recall and or discovery. Without indexes, the searcher would waste time by turning through documents page by page or by examining all items. Indexes save time and make practical searches that would otherwise be given up.
4. Indexes provide, in highly compact form, useful information about a person or field. A general view of a subject area can be obtained from a subject index.
5. The cross-references in the subject indexes guide users to accept facts of a field.
6. Nomenclature, terminology and spelling are often helpfully provided by indexes and their introductions.
7. The organisation of a field of knowledge can be obtained through classified index or from the cross references in an alphabetic subject index.
8. A major reason for indexing is to aid in solving the problem presented by about 80 languages in which material is now published.
9. Indexes facilitate rapid selection of relevant material.

However, indexing should perform certain points such as Recall and Precision. Recall is the retrieval of documents by the system. A user is primarily concerned with obtaining documents that contribute to the satisfaction of his information need. The recall performance of an information retrieval system can be expressed quantitatively by means of a simple ratio. Recall power is an important attribute of a retrieval system yet it is not the only attribute. It is therefore obvious that: A recall figure on its own is no measure of the efficiency of an information retrieval system. The purpose of index is to screen out as many as possible of the unwanted document while holding back as few as possible of the wanted documents.

The two most important factors governing the recall and precision capabilities of an index are: the exhaustivity of the indexing, and the specificity of the index language. Exhaustivity is a measure of the extent to which the subject content of a document is analysed by the indexer. The indexer must decide how many of the concepts which each document is about, are going to be indexed and translated into the language of the system. If we index each document at maximum exhaustivity, we have achieved a maximum recall capability for our index. Specificity is an important element in the index language is how specific it is to be. The specificity of the vocabulary affects the level of precision that the user can achieve in the system. A highly specific index language will allow high precision capabilities in searching but will also tend to reduce recall performance. An index language of low specificity will tend to produce high recall figures but will not allow high precision performance.

STEPS OF INDEXING

Indexing is the process of creating the entries in an index. There are six essential operations involved in this process.

1. Scanning the Collection

As the indexing style grows in inwardness, the process becomes sophisticated. While scanning the documents for indexing efforts are made to include all possible approach points of users and exclude all possibilities that the users may consider trivial.

2. Analysing the Contents

Analysis being based on pre-determined criteria of use of the collection and the index. The book should be first read through as a whole. This is a very useful preliminary step especially if passages are underlined and notes are made as the book is read. The indexer can then size up the approximate amount of attention paid to various subjects the desirability of various references and headings and the necessity for including or omitting references to minor items.

3. Tagging Discrete Items in the Collection with Appropriate Identifiers

The basic purpose of indexing is to match the ideas expressed in a document with the ideas inherent in a chosen heading from a prescribed list of subject headings. This involves identifying and selecting words or phrases. This process of identification, selection and assigning identifiers, labels to a document's thought content facilitates in retrieving specific documents, specific chunks of information and discrete data after they have been stored.

4. Vocabulary Control

The vocabulary (indexing language) exerts a considerable influence on the performance of indexers / IRS. To exercise control, a select list of index terms is prepared for indexing purpose. The outcome of terminology control comes in the form of standard word list or thesaurus showing the terms that are available for indexing and searching, their relations to words that are not to be used and their relations among themselves.

5. Adding Precise Location

Adding to each identifier the precise location within the collection where the item occurs, so that the user may retrieve it with ease.

6. Arrangement of Entries

After preparing entries, they may be arranged

alphabetically, using the entry word (lead word). The alphabetization is usually done word by word. In this step the alphabetically arranged entries are merged and entered for clarity for the purpose of ready use.

The process of indexing does not include the actual production (ex-printing) of the completed index; and that the term is never applied to using an index.

METHODS OF INDEXING

There are five different methods of indexing:

(i) Concept Indexing

The thought contents of a document consist of various concepts. A decision regarding the exact information worthy of indexing is to be taken, which means that in a particular document, certain concepts are to be pinpointed for inclusion in the index. Thus, when index is prepared based on concepts of the document, it is called conceptual indexing.

(ii) Exhaustive Indexing

When the index includes any valid piece of information available in the document, which is likely to warrant retrieval, in order to make it more comprehensive, it results in exhaustive indexing.

(iii) Specific Indexing

Indexes based on subject headings selected from the document, which expresses the specific subject of the discussed topic, co-extensive with the subject, is called specific indexing.

(iv) Syntactic Indexing

An index where the subject heading displays the relationship of various concepts in the document and consequently becomes unusually longer is called syntactic indexing.

(v) Weighted Indexing

The various concepts of a document, according to the relative importance attached to it, are used as indexing terms. The most important concept is used first, then the less important and so on. This method of indexing is called weighted indexing. Thompson says that it is the best way of indexing, as it is able to assign a figure in a scale, to each concept indexed, showing the relative importance of the concept in the document concerned.

An example would make the various methods of indexing clearer:

"UNESCO's documentation activities in India"

Concept Indexing : Documentation activities

Exhaustive Indexing :

(i) UNESCO	as separator
(ii) Documentation Activities	units of
(iii) India	information

Specific Indexing : India, Documentation Activities

Syntactic Indexing : Documentation activities in India

Weighted Indexing :

1.	Documentation Activities	According India
2.	to the	activities attached
3.	UNESCO	to the concepts.

Indexing is in fact no mechanical process. If it is to be of use, it requires thought and consideration in every phase of its construction. From many points of view, the terms 'indexing' and 'subject cataloguing' are synonymous; but indexing implies more specificity and depth of subject analysis. No information system, manual or automated, is complete without indexing and research goes unabated to improve indexing methodology.

REFERENCES

1. Collision, Robert L. *Indexes and Indexing. London: Ernest Benn, 1959.*
2. Ghosh, S.B. and Satpathi, J.N. *Subject Indexing Systems: Concepts, methods and Techniques. Calcutta: Indian Association of Special Libraries and Information Centres, 1998.*
3. Guha, B. *Documentation and information services: techniques and systems. Calcutta: World Press, 1983.*
4. Kent, Allen [et.al.]. *Encyclopaedia of Library and Information Science. New York: Marcel Dekker, 1974, V.II. pp. 186-89.*
5. Khan, M.T.M. *Information Organization and Communication. New Delhi: Ess Ess, 1997-98.*
6. Khanria, J. K. *Communicating Knowledge. Delhi: Research, 1996.*
7. Prasher, R.G. *Index and indexing systems. New Delhi: Medellion Press, 1989.*
8. Rajan, T.N. *Indexing systems: concepts, models and techniques. Calcutta: IASLIC, 1981.*
9. Riaz, Mohammad. *Modern techniques of documentation and information work. Delhi: Royal, 1992.*
10. Rothman, *J. Indexer and Indexing.*
11. Varma, A.K. *Trend in subject indexing. Delhi: Mittal, 1984.*

7

Pre-Coordinate Indexing

Information Retrieval System involves matching the information need of users with items that resolve those needs. Traditionally this meant supplying users with documents but more recently it has involved providing a far wider range of items such as the documents, articles, abstract, bibliographical references etc.

Indexing is the most important component of an IRS. In fact, the very success of an IRS depend upon the quality of indexing. The appropriate and accurate index terms or phrases assigned can retrieve pertinent bits or items of information, where as failure to assign suitable index term or phrases can result in missing the document when required.

The indexing system can be categorized into two types, i.e., Pre-coordinate indexing, and Post-coordinate indexing

PRE COORDINATE INDEXING SYSTEM

The kind of system in which terms are combined or coordinated at the time of indexing by the indexer, is known as Pre-coordinate indexing system. In Pre-coordinate indexing systems documents are search under the same terms which indexer originally assigned to them without any further manipulation of terms at the time of searching.

Pre-coordinate indexing is thus essentially a

conventional method commonly encountered in printed indexes where a document is represented in index by a headings consisting of chain of terms.

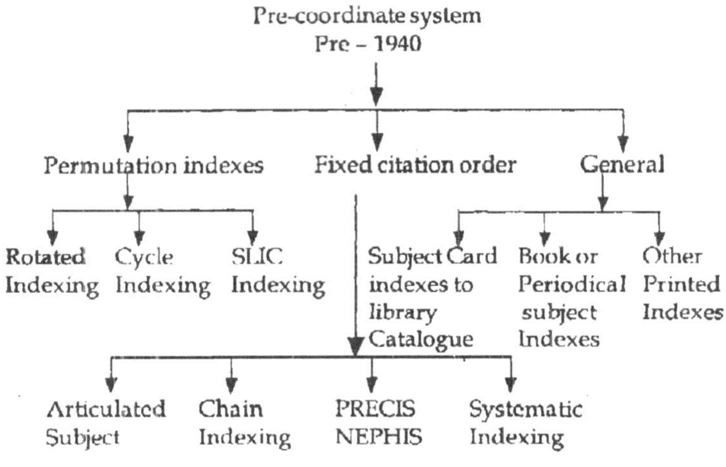

Pre-Coordinate Indexing System

To approach a composite heading via one of the concepts that does not take the first position in the citation order, is a problem that must be considered to provide access to secondary concepts. Some of important techniques are described to solve several problems.

CHAIN INDEXING

Chain indexing, originally called chain procedure is indeed a classic contribution of Ranganathan and proved as most useful technique in Indexing. Encyclopedia of Library & Information Science has defined chain indexing as a "method of deriving alphabetical subject entries in a semi-automatic fashion from the chain of successive subdivision that leads from a general level to the most specific level needed to be indexed".

The chain procedure aims at implementing the policy of subject indexing - grouping by juxtaposition or grouping by referencing as the case may be; and at providing the necessary and sufficient number of points of approach for specific subject. If A, B, C and D are index terms, chain procedure creates the following.

ABCD

BCD

CD

D

Thus, the entries for a document on a "Law concerning corruption in bureaucracy in Pakistan" may be:

Law: Corruption: Bureaucracy: Pakistan

Corruption: Bureaucracy: Pakistan

Bureaucracy: Pakistan Pakistan

PRECIS

Since its inception in 1950, the BNB (British National Bibliography) had adopted chain indexing system of Ranganathan to generate subject index entries and feature headings. In 1971, BNB replaced the chain indexing system by PRECIS, the acronym of Preserved Context Indexing System. Important points are that PRECIS indexing is basically human, the system is not post-coordinate and the permutation not derived from hierarchical classification or notation, could be used in alphabetical cataloguing.

The shunting procedure used in PRECIS would create the entries with A, B, C, D as index terms as given below

(i) A
BCD

(ii) BA
CD

(iii) CBA
D

(iv) DCBA

By using the same example as above, PRECIS would cause entries as:

1. Law
   Corruption Bureaucracy Pakistan
2. Corruption Law
   Bureaucracy Pakistan
3. Bureaucracy Corruption Law
   Pakistan
4. Pakistan Bureaucracy Corruption Law

Other approach to the movement of the components of the index headings in order to generate additional entries are also possible. These techniques are - cycled or cyclic indexing, rotated indexing and SLIC indexing.

Cycled indexing involves the movement of the first lead term to the last position in the subsequent entry. This process repeated untill each concept has occupied the lead position.

ABCD Law : Corruption : Bureaucracy : Pakistan
BCDA Corruption : Bureaucracy : Pakistan : Law
CDAB Bureaucracy :Pakistan : Law : Corruption
DABC Pakistan : Law : Corruption : Bureaucracy

Rotated indexing involves each element in turn becoming the heading under which an entry is filed, but no change in citation order takes place.

ABCD Law : Corruption : Bureaucracy : Pakistan
ABCD Law : Corruption: Bureaucracy : Pakistan
ABCD Law : Corruption : Bureaucracy : Pakistan
ABCD Law : Corruption : Bureaucracy : Pakistan

SLIC (Selective listing in combination) indexing involves the combination of elements, but in one direction only. By applying this technique the following entries are derived:

ABCD Law : Corruption: Bureaucracy : Pakistan
ACD Law : Bureaucracy : Pakistan
AD Law: Pakistan

BCD	Corruption : Bureaucracy : Pakistan
CD	Bureaucracy :Pakistan
D	Pakistan

POPSI (POSTULATE BASED PERMUTED SUBJECT INDEXING)

POPSI was propounded by G. Bhattacharya of DRTC, Bangalore, as an improvement over chain indexing. The main defect of chain indexing was its dependence on a scheme of classification and disappearing chain. These two problems have been eliminated by the POPSI system of subject indexing. POPSI is useful in a number of ways. Some of them are: Formulating subject headings which may be used as feature heading or for other indexing purposes; Deriving subject index entries for a classified catalogue, and to a book etc.; Determining the subject of readers query, in a consistent and helpful way; Formulating a strategy for searching information about a subject in a catalogue; and Deriving a base for the presentation of ideas in the text of a document.

ADVANTAGES OF PRE-COORDINATE INDEXING SYSTEM

Pre-coordinate indexes eliminate the need for a sophisticated search logic (boolean). They require no special features in their physical format. Some of these indexes are totally independent of the computer in formatting and display of entries.

LIMITATIONS OF PRE-COORDINATE INDEXING SYSTEM

In Pre-coordinate Indexing System a particular sequence of coordination of index terms may not meet the approaches of all the users of index file; to overcome this limitation, multiple entry system and a network of references have to be provided. In Pre coordination of index terms may be too broad for a particular search; and the user does not have any freedom to manipulate the coordination of terms in a desired manner to his specific needs.

After going through the types, advantages and limitations of pre-coordinate indexing it is observed that in all pre coordinate indexes the subject description is composed of a set of terms which constitutes a summarisation of the subject. Thus when a user asks for information on a particular compound subject, the combination of concepts involve will be easily matched in an index against an entry for the same combination.

But, the limitations of Pre coordinate indexing and consequent dissatisfaction with its working were responsible for the development of another system i.e., post coordinate indexing system.

REFERENCES

1. Ghosh, S.B. and Satpati, I.N. *Subject indexing system: concepts, methods and techniques. Calcutta: 1ASL1C, 1998.*
2. Khanna, J.K. *Advances in Librarianship; New Delhi: ESS ESS, 1985.*
3. Prasher, R.C. *Index and Indexing system; M.P.: Medallian, 1939.*
4. Rajan, T.N. (ed.). *Indexing system: concept, models and techniques. Calcutta: IASLIC, 1981.*

8

Post-Coordinate Indexing

Sequential scanning of a list of documents to locate a desired item is both difficult and time-consuming if the list happens to be long. This problem can be taken care by providing multiple access through an index, which permits us to go direct to the information required. Providing multiple access through subsidiary sequences which lead to the required items in main sequence is known as an indexing system.

COORDINATE INDEXING

Due to interdisciplinary nature of research, subject indexing is becoming a complicated process. Since most of the documents of present day) cover composite subjects, representation of subject contents with a single index term looked impossible and it called for a combination or coordination of a number of terms. During the process two or more concepts are coordinated to represent a new one, which differs from the individual concepts. Co-ordinate indexing systems for information or document retrieval can broadly be divided into two categories; i.e., Pre-coordinate Indexing System and Post-coordinate Indexing System.

In Pre-coordinate indexing system the coordination of indexing terms is done at the input stage by the indexer.

The indexer combines the indexing terms for each entry in a fixed citation order that is most likely to be preferred by the user, who does not have any freedom to manipulate the coordinate terms in a manner desired by him to satisfy his specific requirement.

Post-coordinate indexing system eliminates the need for combination order by using only single concepts at the input or indexing stage and transferring the act of coordination to the output or searching stage.

CHARACTERISTICS OF POST-COORDINATE INDEXING SYSTEM

In post coordinate indexing systems coordination of index terms is done at the search stage i.e. a number of headings are searched in such a way that documents! have common headings are selected. The main characteristics of post coordinate indexing are:

(i) It is based on subject analysis;

(ii) No fixed citation order is maintained at the time of indexing; and

(iii) The users do coordination of index items at the output or search stage.

The post coordinate indexing system is of two types, i.e., Term Entry system and Item Entry system.

In Term Entry system, a concept is represented as a heading in a term card and accession numbers of all documents carrying that concepts are posted on it. Thus, we need to make as many entries for a document as we select terms to describe its contents. In each of these entries accession numbers of the document will be available in appropriate columns. Uniterm and optical coincidence methods are examples of this system.

Item Entry system is that in which one card is maintained for a document. Each concept relevant to the subject matter of the document is represented in code form by a series of notches punched out from the holes along the margins of the card and the central area of the card is used for document description.

Based on the basic principles of post coordinate indexing, a number of systems have been developed.

1. Uniterm
2. Peek - a -boo
3. Edge - notched card
4. Aperture cards
5. Duel Dictionaries

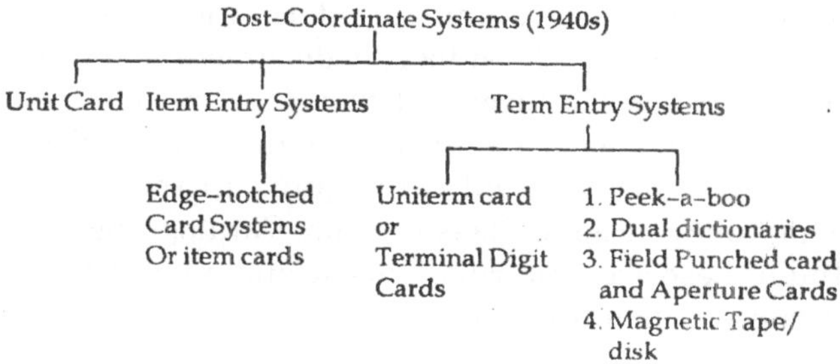

1. UNITERM Indexing System

Uniterm is a combination of two words Unit and Term. Unit stands for a single concept and Term for a single word. Uniterm, therefore means a single word representing a single concept. Uniterm indexing system is a Post coordinate indexing system based on term entry principle. It was developed by Mortimer Taube in 1953. The Uniterm system involves the indexing of documents under single words (uniterms) extracted from the document itself or chosen from a prescribed list of subjects (descriptors).

A Uniterm card has a space at the top for the headings, the rest of the card being divided into 10 vertical columns, headed respectively from 0 to 9 cards are in alphabetical order according to the index term at their head. Each Uniterm used to index documents appear as the heading on a separate (5×8 inch) Uniterm card.

(a) Document Identification Number

Each document to be indexed is given an identification number. This can be the accession number of the document. The accession file is maintained according to these accession number. It also gives necessary bibliographical details about each document.

(b) Finding out Uniterms

A Uniterm is a single word for a single concept. It represents the contents or the ideas or concepts of a document. Uniterms are units of information available in a document. Normally, the subject of document is represented by more than one Uniterm and therefore, such a document is indexed under each Uniterm. For instance, a document entitled Classification and cataloguing in the libraries of India has four concepts. Classification, Cataloguing Libraries and India these are uniterms. This document will be indexed under these four uniterms.

(c) Entry Making

Entry is made in a Uniterm card, the identification numbers of relevant documents are to be entered in the appropriate column, using the terminal digit posting. While preparing the index, appropriate uniterms are decided for the subject of the document to be indexed. The Uniterm cards carrying these uniterms are removed from the pack. If no card is available for a particular Uniterm, a fresh card is prepared. The document identification number is then entered in these Uniterm cards using terminal digit parting. Thus the documents with identification numbers 1118, 2221, 1597, 3462 will be posted in column 8,1,7 and 2 respectively. After the posting of identification numbers, the Uniterm cards are again arranged in the file alphabetically.

(d) Search procedure

The search procedure consists of three steps : analysis of request; lacking out relevant cards; and identifying relevant documents.

When a request for a documents on a particular subject is received, the first step is to analyse the subject and to translate it into appropriate uniterms. The second step to call from the alphabetical file the Uniterm cards representing these uniterms. The final step is to search out the relevant documents by comparing the numbers in the called out cards. When an identification number is found common in these cards, it is accepted that the document represented by that number deals with the subject which the users is searching.

In a document titled Library Training in India', the relevant concepts are Libraries, Training and India.

Libraries

0	*1*	*2*	*3*	*4*	*5*	*6*	*7*	*8*	*9*
		2							
20									
	11	42	213			296	517	388	29
				54	275				
	2221	3462					1597		

Training

0	*1*	*2*	*3*	*4*	*5*	*6*	*7*	*8*	*9*
		52						78	
			63	24		166			
30	111	172						18	
		3462							

India

0	*1*	*2*	*3*	*4*	*5*	*6*	*7*	*8*	*9*
								68	
20		32	63	63		15	87		29
50	151	62	62	43	64				
						296	117	448	99
		3462							

MERITS OF UNITERM INDEXING SYSTEM

Uniterm Indexing System has the following merits:

(i) No classification system is required to organize the documents indexed by Uniterm. These are arranged by their accession numbers.

(ii) As all the documents are arranged according to their accession numbers, retrieving the requisite document is simple and easy.

(iii) The work of the indexing stage is simple as the coordination of the subject components is done at the output stage. There is no problem of citation order at the input stage.

(iv) Since the system is simple and uses natural language, the users can understand it without difficulty and can make use of it easily.

(v) The physical size of the index can be kept within manageable limits by a accommodating a number of items in a single Uniterm card.

LIMITATIONS OF UNITERM INDEXING SYSTEM

Some of the limitations of this systems are:

(i) The limitation of the card size only a limited number of documents can be entered on a single Uniterm card.

(ii) Direct approach to the documents is not possible since they are not arranged in a systematic order.

(iii) The simplicity of using keywords from title is more apparent than real i.e. ambiguity of terms; synonymous, near synonymous and variable constructions; and generic to specific relationships create real difficulties.

(iv) In some cases, there is false coordination in this system. The coordination of two uniterms British and Indian, may yield documents on the British Indian and Indian British i.e., two different subjects.

2. PEEK - A - BOO or Opticle Coincidence System

The first satisfactory Post-coordinate systems were introduced in the 1940's by Batter in England and Cordonnier in France. The principle used has been given many names including "feature cards", but it is commonly known and referred to as "peek-a-boo" or the "opticle coincidence cards".

One way of making searching easier *is* to translate number into positions, indicating the presence of number on a card by punching out a hole at its position. To search, hold the relevant cards up to the light, which will shine through those positions which are punched out on all the cards being held.

A peek-a-boo card contains a space at the top for the heading like a Uniterm card, but the body of the card is divided up into numbered squares. A small card will probably contain 500 or 1,000 positions, while a large one will contain upto 10,000. To enter information into the system, we select the term we require to describe a document, and remove these card from the file; then using a punch we drill out a hole in the position corresponding to the document number and refile the cards in their alphabetical order.

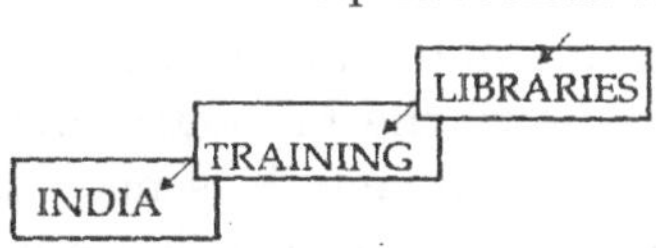

During the search the cards representing the components of the query are taken out of the file, put together duly aligned and place before source of light. The common holes on all the cards will permit the light to pass through them revealing the identification of the documents dealing with the subject of query. The search operation in this system is comparatively speedy.

3. EDGE - NOTCHED Cards System

This system belongs to the category of item entry system. For the former system, one index card is to be prepared for each component of the subject of the document.

But in this system one card is maintained for a document. Each concept relevant to the subject matter of the document is represented in code form by a series of notched punched out from the holes along the margin of the cards. And the central area of these cards is used for document description.

Concepts	Code	Document
Libraries	1	Description
Periodicals	4	
Classification	6	

Before the search is started the user should know the code number assign to the subject of query. Then with the help of a needle he can separate the notched cards. The needle is inserted at a relevant position passing through the file of cards. The card which have their holes intact will stay on the needle and those whose edges have been notched will fall down when the needle is raised. By repeating the sorting operation, the card notched at a given position or combination of positions are separated from the card which are not notched at these positions. The notched cards represent the documents on the subject of query and may also contain abstract of its contents.

This system has many advantages. Since the central area of each card shows the bibliographical description of the documents, no second search is necessary for knowing the bibliographical details of a document in this system. Operating cost is also low.

The limitation of coding space in the margin of the card is the only serious drawback of this system. The entire file is to be scanned in this system for any query.

4. Aperture Cards

These are a special form of marginal storage cards which permits the entire document to be stored in the centre of the card. A microform insert which contains the full text of the document being indexed is more than an index, it is a complete document collection and cards must be withdrawn in order to read documents. Aperture cards are a useful form of storing technical drawings and have been used to store and retrieve patents.

5. Dual Dictionaries

Dual dictionaries are printed computer produced post-coordinate indexes. These are not card based. Two identical lists are printed on continuous computer stationary. In each list index terms are arranged alphabetically and document numbers are listed under each index term. Numbers are usually grouped in columns according to their terminal digit. Search is made by comparing the numbers entered under two or more index terms. A dual dictionary can be produced in multiple copies like printed catalogue. However, searching is tedious and prone to error.

In spite of the deficiencies that might occur is post coordinate system, their merits proclaim them to be an effective device for information retrieval. There is no problem of citation order involved and no classification system is required to organize the document indexed. The systems are simple, using natural language and are very flexible, enabling the user to either broader or narrow the search very easily. The user can readily manipulate the search towards seeking to satisfy his own particular information needs. Hence, post-coordinate indexing systems are extremely search effective.

REFERENCES

1. Ghosh, S.B. and Satpathi, J.N. *Subject indexing systems: Concepts, Methods and Techniques. Calcutta: IASLIC, 1998.*
2. Guha, B. *Documentation and information: services, techniques and systems, Calcutta: World, 1983.*
3. Khan, M.T.M. *Information, Organization and Communication. New Delhi: ESS ESS, 1997-98.*
4. Khanna, J.K. *Communicating Knowledge. Delhi: Research.*
5. Parasher, R.G. *Index and Indexing system. New Delhi: Medallion, 1989.*
6. Riaz, Muhammad, *Modern Techniques of documentation and information work. New Delhi: Royal, 1992.*

9

Chain Indexing

Chain Indexing originally called Chain Procedure is a great landmark in the history of Pre-coordinate indexing. It was developed, christened and systematized by S.R. Ranganathan. It was fostered in practice, mainly by E.J. Coates, in the subject part of B.N.B.'s (British National Bibliography) index, and now it is accepted by many classified cataloguers as the single best way of constructing a subject indexing economically and usefully. In the chain procedure, the expressive name of a specific subject is represented in terms of its fundamental components, the sequence of which is determined by a set of postulates and principles. Each component is standardized. The chain having the name of subject in standard term as the last link, is determined. Distinction is made between sought, unsought and false links. A subject heading is derived from each of the sought links in the chain according to a set of rules formulated to suit the purpose in hand.

Encyclopaedia of Librarianship has defined chain indexing as a semi-mechanical method. G. Bhattacharya defines chain indexing as "any systematic method of divising subject headings for specific subject involving the determination of chain in which the subject concerned is the last sought link. Encyclopaedia of Library and Information

Science has defined chain indexing as a 'method of deriving alphabetical subject index entries in a semi-automatic fashion from the chain of successive subdivision that leads from a general level to the most specific level needed to be indexed. Ranganathan defines the chain procedure as procedure for deriving subject word entry from a class number in a more or less mechanical way. This method is used to derive class index entries in classified catalogue, and specific subject entries, subject analyticals and "see also" subject entries in dictionary catalogue.

Chain procedure is the methodology of deriving subject headings for a specific compound subject, which involves the determination of the chain in which subject concerned is the last link. In simple words - chain indexing is based on a logical correlation between classification and cataloguing. Chain indexing is the hyphen that joins the buckle that fastens classification and alphabetical subject indexing.

PRE-REQUISITES FOR CHAIN INDEXING

The chain procedure works successfully and efficiently on the following conditions:

The book must be classified first and catalogued later. It means that a book would be read technically by the classifier and not by the cataloguer. The class number allotted to the book should be co-extensive, i.e. it should represent the specific subject of the book, through a proper and befitting class number. Classification scheme adopted for classification of document should be well modulated. Though faceted classification scheme is more appropriate for deriving chain, however, it is not impossible in case of enumerative scheme of classification. The term denoting the class number should be general and currently in use.

There are four important links, while functioning with the chain procedure, viz.,

(i) **False Link** is that link which ends with a connecting symbol in the class number. Links ending with a digit representing a phase relation, an intra-phase relation, or an intra-array phase relation and the time isolate representing time itself in the facet are also treated as false link.

(ii) Unsought Link is that link which ends with a part of the isolate focus (any idea and also the number and name representing it) in a class number; and also represents a subject on which reading material is not likely to be produced or sought or which is not likely to be looked up by any reader seeking materials on specific subject forming last link of the following class number.

(iii) Missing Link is a link in a chain with gap corresponding to the missing isolate in the chain. In representing a class number in the form of a chain, every missing link is to be inserted at a proper place whenever there is such a need.

(iv) All remaining links are Sought Links.

STEPS INVOLVED IN CHAIN INDEXING

Bhattacharya enumerates nine steps involved in the chain procedure, which are explained here under.

(1) Determination of the specific subject of the document,

(2) Naming of the specific subject of the document expressively in the natural languages,

(3) Name of the subject in Kernel Terms i.e. in terms of its fundamental components,

(4) Determination of the category of each fundamental component according to a set of postulates and principles formulated for this purpose.

(5) Transformation of the analyzed name-of-subject by rearranging, if necessary, the fundamental components according to a few additional postulates and principles formulated,

(6) Name of the subject in standard terms,

(7) Determination of each of the links of the chain in which the subject denoted by the name of subject in standard terms is the last link (determination of upper links).

(8) Determination of the different kinds of links, such as sought link, unsought link, false link and missing link (determination of kinds of link), and

(9) Derivation of a subject heading from each of the sought links in the chain according to a set of rules formulated to suit the purpose at hand (derivation of subject headings).

The actual operation of chain indexing can be studied with the help of following example: supposing the document is on "Nationalization of Banks in India". The indexer will analyze the contents of the document and translate this (according to (Colon Classification, ed. 6, rev.) into the following formulation in the light of nine steps enumerated above:

Step I — Specific subject: Nationalization of Banks in India

Step II — Expressive name of the subject: Nationalization of banks in India in Economics

Step III — Kernel terms: Nationalization. Banks. India. Economics

Step IV — Analyzed name of the subject: Nationalization (Spl.) Banks (P) India (S) Economics (BC)

Step V — Transformed title: Economics (BC) Banks (P), Public Enterprise (Spl.) India (S)

Step VI — Standard terms: Economics (BC) Banks (P) Public Enterprise (Spl) India (S)

Step VII — Determination of upper links: X (BC) 62(P), 9W (Spl.) 44(S)

This analysis is translated into the notation of the Colon Classification 6th rev. ed.

Step VIII — Determination of kinds of links: Classified Index Entry.

Chain Structure

X	Economics (sought link)
X9W	Public Enterprise, Economics (Sought Link)
X9W	False Link
X9W,6	Credit, Public Enterprise, Economics (Unsought link)
X9W,62	Banks, Public Enterprise, Economics (Unsought link)
X9W,62.4	Asia, Public Enterprise, Banks, Asia (Sought link)
X9W,62.44	India, Banks, Public Enterprise, Economics

Step IX Derivation of subject headings:

India, Banks, Public Enterprises, Economics	X9W,62.44
Banks, Public Enterprise, Economics	X9W,62
Public Enterprise, Economics	X9W
Economics	X

Chain indexing can also be operated with any scheme of classification. Here is an example worked out with Dewey Decimal Classification Scheme.

The document entitled "Paraffins" with class number 547.11 generates the following chain:

500	Science	(Unsought Link)
540	Chemistry	(Sought Link)
547	Organic Chemistry	(Sought Link)
547.	False Link	
547.4	Aliphatic Compound Organic Chemistry	(Unsought Link)
547.41	Hydrocarbons	(Sought Link)
547.41	Paraffins (Organic Chemistry)	(Sought Link)

The above chain has seven links in all. Out of these, one is a false link, two are unsought links, and four are sought links. Corresponding to the sought links, there are four subject headings or class index entries as follows:

Paraffins, Organic Chemistry	547.411
Hydrocarbons, Organic Chemistry	547.41
Organic Chemistry	547
Chemistry	540

MERITS AND DEMERITS OF CHAIN INDEXING

Chain Indexing has the following merits:

1. The classifier analyzes the subject of the document to have a structural formulation of the subject as its class number. The indexer starts from this stage and retranslates the class number to provide alphabetical approach through class index entries. Chain indexing thus saves the duplication of work.
2. Chain indexing is based on the classification number and the terminology given in the schedules. It is therefore, semi-mechanical as also a speedy procedure.
3. Irrespective of the scheme of classification, subject headings or class index entries can be derived from class number with the help of chain indexing.
4. For a string having four components, only four subject headings are made according to chain indexing, through the permutation of four terms would have given 24 headings. This system thus brings in tremendous economy.
5. Chain indexing provides alternative approach to the classified file through reverse rendering. It is helpful to the users in retrieving their information.
6. DRTC has found the chain procedure fully amenable to computerization. Programs were successfully written to generate subject headings both from class numbers and feature headings following a conventional reverse rendering method.

7. Chain procedure may also be used to derive indexes to classification schemes and books. It may be used in formulation headings necessary for guide cards in a catalogue, stack room guides, gangway guides, bay guides, shelf guides, etc. in a consistent way.
8. Each word got by the chain indexing may not be a sought heading.
9. Sought and Unsought links make it less mechanical

Apart from the above stated merits, chain indexing has got some limitations. These are:

1. Out of the subject headings generated for a document through chain indexing, only the last one is specific and other represent broader subjects. The specific subject heading shall be available to only that user who has a particular search formulation. The problem of the disappearing chain lands us in this situation.
2. Besides the generic entries, chain indexing may also generate some entries for empty links in the chain in the case of a document of a highly specialized field. These empty links create noise in the file.
3. As chain indexing uses the class number for drawing subject headings, its efficiency or otherwise depends on the scheme of classification. A procedure dependent on the scheme of classification has to share the defects of that scheme; and
4. There is a problem of missing links in chain indexing.

Chain indexing, originally called chain procedure, is indeed a classic contribution of Ranganathan. There is no doubt that considerable work has been done on it, and the achievements also are quite significant. The results of the investigations on the chain indexing have successfully established that the denotation of this concept is considerably extensive, and its connotation fairly intensive.

REFERENCES

1. Ghosh, S.B. and Satpathi, J.N. ed. *Subject Indexing Systems, concepts methods and techniques. Calcutta: IASLIC, 1998.*
2. Guha, B. *Documentation and Information : Services, techniques and systems. Calcutta: World Press, 1983.*
3. Khanna, J.K. *Communicating Knowledge. Delhi: Research,1996.*
4. Ramkrishnan, M.N. *Indexing Systems and Techniques. Trivendrum: Lakshmishree, 1986.*
5. Verma, A.K. *Tends in Subject Indexing. Delhi: Mittal, 1984.*

10

Citation Indexing

Information retrieval systems involve matching of information needs of users with items that resolve those needs. The role of information retrieval systems in libraries or information units, therefore, is to inform the users on the existence (or non-existence) and where abouts of documents demanded by him at the moment. In this context, indexing is the most important component of information system. In fact, the very success of information system depends upon the quality of indexing. Appropriate and accurate index terms assigned can retrieve pertinent items of information, whereas failure to assign suitable index terms can result in missing the document when required. The development of so many indexing techniques closely reflects this idea.

INDEXES AND INDEXING

The word index derived from the Latin word 'indicare' meaning to indicate or point out. According to Allen Kent, an index is "a device that serves as a pointer or indicator, must often an alphabetic list that includes subjects and names of people or places that are considered to be of special pertinence in a graphic record." An index consists of a series of entries appearing, not in the order in which they appear in the publication, but in some order (eg. alphabetical) chosen to enable the user to find them quickly, together with references to show where each item is located. It has three essential elements; viz., names or terms or concepts constituting index entry; location symbol for each index entry; and arrangement of index entries.

Thus an index is a systematically arranged guide giving enough information about each item to enable to be a link between a specific subject or topic and the identified document. In simple terms, indexing is the art and science of preparing an index. Indexing as an art anticipates the use of sense and taste and as a science appreciates the use of rules and patterns. It has been defined as "the process of analysing the information content of recorded knowledge and expressing this information content in the language of indexing system" (Brenner, 1979) or "regarded as the fact of describing or identifying a document in terms of subject content." (UNISIST, 1975)

TYPES OF INDEXING

One can identify various types of indexing based on the characteristic chosen from division. For example:

By Co-ordination, one can identify them as Pre-coordinate Indexing (Context-Specifying indexing) and Post-coordinate Indexing (Content-free indexing)

By Permutation (Title) the following types can be identified: Keyword in Context (KWIC); Keyword Out of Context (KWOC); Keyword Augmented in Context (KWAC); Keyword with Context (KWWC); and Key-term Alphabetical (KEYTALPHA).

Traditional indexing systems suffer from a number of serious limitations, important among these being - notation or subject headings are sometimes ambiguous, having altogether different meanings, leading to the problem of semantics and vocabulary control. It is difficult for subject labels to keep pace with the rate of growth of subjects; being subject oriented, traditional indexing has limited utility in supporting multi-disciplinary research. The tremendous growth of literature and the availability of limited number of indexers result in a serious time lag; and Indexers having different capabilities, the same document may be indexed differently by different indexers.

These problems leading to a search for a better indexing system, the Citation Indexing System was introduced to overcome the limitations inherent in traditional indexing processes.

CITATION INDEXING

In traditional subject indexing, an inverted file of all the document *is* constructed on the basis of a subject term. However, Citation Indexing (CI) represent an entirely new approach to the problem of file organization since it does not depend for its indexing technique either upon word derivations from text or upon word assignment. A citation index is an ordered list of cited articles, each of which is accompanied by a list of citing articles. The citing article *is* identified as a source, the cited articles as a reference.

Citation Indexing is based on the assumption that: An author's references (citation) to previously published documents indicate the existence of a subject relationship between the current publication and the older publications; and Document that cite the same publications usually have subject relationship with each others.

In other words, a citation implies a relationship between a part or the whole of a cited paper and part or the whole of the citing paper by following the subsequent citations, the history of an idea can be treated where and how it has been applied and whether it is sustained, rejected or absorbed into later works.

Citation Indexing techniques thus overcomes the problem of semantics and vocabulary control, since it is independent of subject terms. Through Citation Indexing it is possible to approach a subject through the author or title by linking the two and taking them as chains in subject linkage. In fact, it treats the author as a subject and builds a chain that is unending.

ESSENTIAL FEATURES OF CITATION INDEXING

Simple : The involvement of human indexers in the compilation of other indexes makes it time consuming and naturally, its cost increases. Whereas the citation indexing is quicker and its compilation is simple as it does not involve the services of indexers.

Effective and Stable : It enables to find out largest possible number of relevant papers. Search efficiency is concerned with minimizing the retrieval of irrelevant papers. Depth of indexing is the primary quantitative measure of search effectiveness. As indexing depth increases, the probability to satisfy the needs of the user also increases.

No language bar : The need for knowing the language to index a document is avoided in Citation Indexing. Documents in different languages get indexed in its most appropriate place automatically.

Ability to cross subject boundaries and time : Any subject index covers the literature of specific subject or group of subjects viz. Mathematics, Chemistry, Physics with in a specified time frame and it imposes these limits on the scope of its indexing terms. Whereas a citation index is prepared from the literature of a limited number of disciplines within a given time frame, the citations, it would use as indexing statements would not be bound by these limits. The citations cross disciplinary nature enable the index to more back ward and forward in time.

Extensive time search : A citation index search can start at any point in time at which a pertinent paper on the subject was published. If that paper is cited during the year covered by the Index, the searcher will get most of the information. Then, he can use the recent papers to cycle back in time to the publication dates of their citations. Thus, a searcher can offer use a single edition of a citation index to obtain a view of the historical development of a subject.

STEPS INVOLVED IN CITATION INDEXING

Citation Indexing involves the following steps :

(1) Deciding the coverage : At the outset a decision is taken about the subject, the period to be covered and the specific documents the citation of which are to be indexed. Although periodical are usually" taken up for citation indexing, other primary documents like conference proceedings, patents, standards, research papers and even books may be covered, if necessary.

(2) Scanning source documents : The selected source documents are then scanned, relevant articles or section identified and their citations checked. If a citation is found incomplete or doubtful, the cited document may be consulted and the citation concerned be completed or rectified.

(3) Preparation of entry : An entry is made for each citation on a standard sized card or slip, each entry consisting of essential details of the cited documents and those of the citing document. An indication about the citing documents, i.e. whether it is an article (review, abstract or original) or a standard or a patent etc. is also given in the entry. Sometimes code numbers are used for indicating cited and citing documents.

(4) Sorting of entries : All the entries thus prepared are sorted out by cited documents or their code numbers. This yields a bunch of entries for each cited documents.

(5) Consolidation of entries : Each bunch of entries is then consolidated so that the details of the citing documents are arranged in some order, usually alphabetical by their authors names and placed along with the details of the cited document, which is common to the bunch.

(6) Arrangement of entries : Each consolidated entry consisting of the details of a cited document and those of its citing documents is arranged in some convenient order, usually alphabetical by the names of the cited authors.

(7) Preparation of indexes : For the user's convenience, some indexes like index of the citing or source documents, index of the topics covered by the documents, the citation of which have been indexed, etc. may be compiled.

(8) Press copy making : If the Citation Index *is* to be printed, the press copy is prepared by typing it out and offering necessary instructions to the press.

The idea of a Citation Index is not new. Shepard's Citation Index has been gainfully employed since 1873, in the legal profession. It is still being published and is an indispensable tool for lawyers. Citation Index has been tremendously successful in law since much of it is based on precedents. As an inventory, the citation Index collects at one place bibliographical descendants of a given cited case enabling the searcher in legal literature to be led automatically from a given case of reference to several later cases which may have influenced in modifying its result or in deciding the later cases. Citation Indexes are also available in the field of Genetics, Statistics, Radio Engineering and one covering all sciences.

EXAMPLE ILLUSTRATING THE USE OF CITATION INDEXES

Let us say for e.g., that a person/aware of S.R. Ranganathan's Chain Procedure as spelled out in his work Classified Catalogue Code (1945) and is interested to know if someone has tested this technique and for whether it has been commented upon by others in the field. It is difficult to conduct search in subject indexes that have to be approached by words - subject headings, key-words, concepts etc., the probability is that such subject indexes will not list relevant commentaries under the name 'Ranganathan Chain Indexing'. On the other hand, researchers who have used Ranganathan's technique or who are commenting on it are likely to refer to his document. Hence a Citation Index facilitates the location of documents on this subject. Eg.

CITED DOCUMENT

- Ranganathan, S.R. Classified Catalogue Code. 2nd ed (Madras Library Association, 1945)
- Bhattacharya, G. "Relative Index and Chain Procedure", Library Science Documentation, 8,369 (1971).
- Neelameghan, A, "Chain Procedure and Micro Subjects," Library Science Documentation 5,152 (1968).
- Coates, E.J., "Chain Procedure; Application in British Technology Index", Electro-technology, 8(1), 33 (1964).
- Doughty, D.W. "Chain Procedure Subject Indexing and featuring a classified catalogue", LAR, 57,141 (1955).

The full bibliographic citation, coupled with a reference to the paper in which the citation appeared, recorded in machine processible form, permits ready manipulation by computer to produce listings ready for human consultations.

SIGNIFICANCE OF CITATION INDEX

By virtue of its different construction, citation index tends to bring together material that would never be collected by the usual subject indexing. It is best described as an association of ideas index. If one considers the book as the macro unit of thought and the periodical article as the micro unit of thought, then the citation index in some respect deals in the sub micro or molecular unit of thought. 'Thought' indexes can be extremely useful if they are properly conceived and developed. Comparing the citation index with the subject index, Garfield writes that "The citation Index helps to overcome the problem of changing terminology, time and other inherent limitations of a priori indexing. Citations are permanent and unique, as are the works they identify. The significance of men's writings may change, but their identities are fixed".

SOME IMPORTANT CITATION INDEXES

(i) Science Citation Index, Philadelphia, Institute for Scientific Information, 1961. 6 Issues per year.

(ii) Social Science Citation Index, Philadelphia, Institute of Scientific Information, 1969. 6 issues per year.

SCIENCE CITATION INDEX

Science citation index is the best known and most commonly used citation index. It is the only regularly published index in science and technology. Currently, it covers about 3300 primary journals, which are published world over, it also includes articles, short communications, letter, reviews, discussions, conference items etc. The frequency of SCI is quarterly and December issue is a cumulative issue for the whole year.

Initially, SCI started with two parts - Citation Index and Source Index. Since 1967, its third part Permuterm Subject Index was introduced.

CITATION INDEX

The Citation Index is arranged alphabetically by cited author. Each cited entry contains the names of the cited author, the year of publication of the item, the name of the host document in which the cited item was published along with its volume and pages. If there is more than one cited item for any author, these are arranged chronologically by cited year.

Under each cited item is given the source item citing it. The source items are arranged alphabetically by source author's name, name of the host document in which item is published, year of publication, volume number and pages as these help locate the relevant item. Only the first author for both the cited and citing items are given. There is a coded number/ symbol identifying whether the citing item is an article, abstract, editorial etc. Cited items may be recorded from any recorded year, citing items, however, are always from the current year.

CITATION INDEX PART

Cited Author - KOHARAY

Cited Paper	87	Cell	50	495	
Koharav	Aramayo	Genetics	122	65	89
	Fan JB	NUCL ACID	17	2801	89
	Nelieman CJ	Gene	77	185	89 N
	Stirling CJ	Embo J	8	1623	89
Current	Wood ER	IBI01 Chem	264	8297	89
author who	Citing Author's	Journal	Vol.	Starting	Publication
have cited	Name	Title	No.	Page No.	Year

The above illustration shows that article by Y Kohara published in the year 1987 in the periodical Cell, Volume 50, page 495 has been cited in 5 articles by R. Aramayo, J.B. Fan, Nelieman, C.J. Stirling and E.R. Wood and their respective bibliographical details are also given. The document code (N) indicates that the citing item is a note (kind of item).

SOURCE INDEX

It is actually an alphabetical list of all source (citing) items processed for the SCI. Each entry provides the names of joint authors (upto 10), the full title of the citing items, journal title i.e. the title of the host document, volume issue, page, year, type of item and number of references in the bibliography of the source item.

SOURCE INDEX PART

Citing Author	WOODER
Co-author	MATSON SW - The Molecular Cloning of the Gene Encoding the
& Article Title	Escherichia - Coli 75-KDA Helicase and the determination of its Nucleotide-Sequence and Genetic Map Position U 5453
Journal Author	IBIOL CHEM 264(14): 8297-8303 89 54R

Autnor Address Univ Carolina, Dept Biol, Chapel Hill, NC 27599, USA

The above mentioned illustration shows that W.R. Wood with the collaboration of S.W. Matson published a paper in the "Journal of Biological Chemistry" in the year 1989 which appeared on pages 8297- 8303 of volume 264, issue 14. The full title of this paper is also given. It also shows that it contains fifty four references. U5453 is the accession number.

The Source Index has a separate section called Corporate Index. It lists all items processed under the organization where the work was performed, indicating under each organization. The names of authors, source journals, volume and page.

CORPORATE INDEX PART

NORTH CAROLINA

CHAPEL HILL

UNIV N CAROLINA

DEPT BIOL

GHOSHS	EMBOJ	8	1191	89
SAUNDERS DS	PNAS US	86	3748	89
WOOD ER	J BIOL CHEM	264	8297	89
Citing Author	Journal Title	Vol. No.	Starring Page	Year

Department of Biology, University of North California is the organization where the citing author E.R. Wood performed the research and published his paper in the Journal of Biological Chemistry, Volume 264, starting page no. 8297 in the year 1989.

PERMUTERM SUBJECT INDEX

The third major index of SCI is the Permuterm Subject Index. It is produced by a Computer which permutes all significant words within each title and sub title of every item included in the source index. It uses the searching technique of following citation/ foot notes in the relevant papers. The PSI is arranged alphabetically by primary term with identical co-terms. For anonymous entries, the journal title is given in place of the author's name.

MOLECULAR-CLONING

GENE	COONEYA
	HOFFMAN E
	MURAT
	WOODER
	ZHOUC
[Genetic Map	WOODER]
Co term	Source author (full information on articles can be found in the source index).

For all those items, when you do not have a name but you do have a specific subject; you can locate bibliographic information with the PSI. As your areas of interest are 'Molecular Cloning' and 'Mapping of Genes' you are required to search the PSI with these items or phrases, and the PSI would refer you to the names of authors who have used these terms in their article titles.

ONLINE AND CD VERSION OF SCI

The on-line version of SCI is known as SCI Search. It contains data from 1974 to date. It is updated bi-weekly and is available through several of the major on-line host systems such as DIALOG etc.

Now, SCI is available in CD also. It incorporates a new feature called related records which leads the searcher to other records having references in common with the ones he has already retrieved.

SOCIAL SCIENCES CITATION INDEX (SSCI)

It is a multidisciplinary index to the literature published in the world's leading 1400 literature in the social sciences. It covers almost all the social science subjects; viz., Anthropology, Business, Education, Geography, History,

Information Science, Law, Philosophy, Sociology, Library Science, Linguistics etc.

The importance of SSCI lies in the fact that it not only links the social disciplines, but it also links them to the so-called natural sciences. It covers selected relevant items from 3,100 science journals.

SSCI appears 3 times a year and has a calendar year index. Each annual cumulation which is available within four months of the end of the year covers all material published during the year.

SEARCH SYSTEM

With four integrated indexes, it is possible to have four completely different access routes to the vast amount of bibliographic data within the SSCI. So, when you are starting a search with limited information, one index leads you to author, and fills in the missing information.

CITATION INDEX

This part of SSCI is arranged alphabetically by cited author. The entry for the cited item carries name and initials of the first author (in case of many), year of publication of the cited item and details like volume and page number of source. The title of the source periodical is represented in abbreviated form. When different papers of a particular author are cited, the papers are arranged in chronological order.

When a particular document cited by different authors in different places, all these citing items are displayed immediately under the cited item. In this case, authors are arranged in an alphabetical order. Coded symbols are A (Abstract), D (Discussion), E (Editorial), L (letters), M (abstracts from meetings), N (Technical notes) are used to indicate the nature of the citing items.

		Pub. Year	Journal Name	Vol. No.	Page No.	Year
Cited author	Daniel AE	84	JP Psychiat	12	527	
Cited Paper		Law				
Current author	Boehnert CE		Law Human B	13	31	89
who have Cited	Denno DW		UPA Lawre	137	615	88
this work	Larkin EP		Med Sci Law	29	26	89
	Cited Author's Name					

CI lists by first author all previously published items that have been cited during the current year just like the SCI.

SOURCE INDEX

Source Index is a straight forward author index to all items published in the journals covered during the year and to items published in other journals whose citations have revealed a link with social sciences. The fields in the source index are same as in the SCI with a "Citation abstract".

Citing Author	Boehnert CR
Article Title	Characteristics of Successful and Unsuccessful Insanity Pleas
Journal	Law Human B Vol. 13, issue no. 1, page 31-39, year of pub. 89 no. of references 16, UO 323 accession no.
Author Address	Univ Minnesota, SCH Med.ep., Psychiat, Box 393, Mayo Bldg Dept, 420 Delaware St SE MinneaPolis, MN, 55455, USA

PERMUTERM SUBJECT INDEX (PSI)

Permuterm is a combination of the words 'Permuted' and 'term'. The term permuted is used in its proper mathematical sense. Accordingly, a title containing 'n' significant words, there will be n(n-1) pairs. This arrangement brings all the terms in primary and co-term position.

	INSANITY	
Co Term	BIAS	BECKHAN JC
	CHARACTERISTICS	BOEHNERT CE
	JURORS	FINKEL NJ
	PLEAS	BOEHNERT CE
		Source author (full information on articles can be found in the SI)

CORPORATE INDEX

If the user does not know any specific article or author and does not have confidence in the vocabulary, even then, if he knows an organization that specializes in research on the subject, that can be used as an entry point in the corporate index. Here he will find the names of people at the institution who have recently published articles. A look up in the SI will provide complete bibliographic information.

MINNESOTA MINNEAPOLIS
UNIV MINNESOTA
SCH MED
DEPT PSYCHIAT
BOX 393

BOEHNERT CR	LAW HUMAN B	13	31	89
Citing Author	Journal	Vol	Starring No.	Year Page

ON-LINE VERSION

The online version of SSCI, Social Sci search provides faster precise searches of the social science literature. Weekly updates make this the most current multi-disciplinary database one can find. Files are available from 1972 to the present. It is available through database vendors like DIALOG etc.

SSCI ON CD

For lighting fast search results and in-depth perspective on the social sciences literature, ISI offers free

90 day trial programme of the SSCI CDE. SSCI CD editions are available individually for the year 1986 to 1991. A 5 year Cummulation covering 1981-85 is also available.

MERITS AND DEMERITS OF CITATION INDEXING

Citation indexing has the following merits:

1. Since no intellectual activity is involved in the compilation of a citation index, its compilation is mechanical using in-built relations of citing and cited documents. This also makes it amenable to mechanization. These two factors contribute towards its prompt publication, reducing the time lag between the reporting of information in the primary journals and its inclusion in the citation index considerably.
2. Citation index is unaffected by changing terminology or new concepts.
3. Citation indexes coverage is multi-disciplinary.
4. Citation index facilitates quicker and easier searching of relevant materials than other conventional indexes.
5. Unlike conventional indexes, citation index ensures that the system is constantly being upgraded by current information, which in turn help to bring old information up-to-date.
6. It helps to find out the core periodicals in a given subject.
7. Citation index is capable of being self organizing. Since each new reference to an old paper and each new citation modifies the previous store of information.

Citation indexes have got some limitations also, viz.,

1. While a conventional index provides a logical subject arrangement, which is helpful to users, a citation index does not provide such an arrangement.
2. Citation index suffers from the problem of starting point, i.e. to begin the search in a citation index, at least one pertinent reference should be known.

3. A citation index does not specify the nature of the relationship a cited document has with the citing documents. There is therefore a remote possibility that the retrieved document do not deal with the subject of the search.
4. A citation index retrieves related documents only and not their contents.
5. Since it is not possible that an author has consulted all the cited documents. Some highly relevant documents might be missed without which a citation index remains incomplete.
6. A citation index according to some critics does not satisfy the exhaustive approach of a user.

With distinct advantages over conventional indexing techniques, citation indexing has emerged as a powerful tool for bibliographical control of micro documents. However, it does not involve retrieval of a great deal of 'noisy' information. Given proper attention, citation indexing has the potential of performing important 'evaluative analytical and predictive roles' in the scientific technological and academic fields.

REFERENCES

1. Guha, B. *Documentation and Information. Calcutta: World Press, 1983.*
2. Khan, M.T.M. *Organization and Communication. New Delhi: Ess Ess, 1997-98.*
3. Khanna, J.K. *Communicating Knowledge. Delhi: Research,!996.*
4. Krishna Kumar. *Reference Service. New Delhi: Vikas, 1994.*
5. Parasher, R.G. *Index and indexing system. New Delhi:Medallion, 1989.*
6. Riaz, Muhammad. *Modern techniques of documentation and information work, Delhi: Royal, 1992.*

11

Preserved Context Indexing System (PRECIS)

PRECIS has been developed by Derek Austin in late sixties as a result of long research which the Classification Research Group under took to give a new general classification for information control. This system is considered as the most important development in alphabetical approach to subject specification in recent years.

The BNB since its inception in 1950 had been using Ranganathan's chain procedure for preparing its alphabetical index (class index entries). The involvement in BNB in the MARC project led it to the exchange of data on magnetic tapes on reciprocal basis with the Library of Congress. Chain procedure did not work well in combination with Decimal Classification in generating the subject index entries directly from the machine readable records. This required a new system to provide alphabetical access to BNB. Some kind of indexing system, independent of classification scheme and capable of representing the contents of a document fully, was needed. Keeping this in view, PRECIS was developed as an improvement on chain procedure.

Derek Austin has defined PRECIS as a system "in which the initial string of terms, organized according to a scheme of role operators, is computer manipulated so that selected words function in turn as the approach term. Entries are restructured at every step in such a way that the user can determine from the lay out of the entry which terms set the appropriate term into its context and which terms are context dependent on the approach term".

OBJECTIVES OF PRECIS

PRECIS has been developed keeping in view the following objectives:

1. The system is to be independent of any scheme of classification.
2. The subject headings to be generated by the system are to be co-extensive with the contents of the document at all access point,
3. The index entries generated by the system are to be meaningful so as to enable the users to interpret them correctly. The system is to avoid unnatural entries and invented headings.
4. After the intellectual job of subject formulation is done, the system is to be amenable to the use of computer for generating additional index entries.
5. The system is to provide an adequate arrangement of references between sematically related terms.
6. The system is to be quite flexible so as to accommodate freely new terms being put into the literature.

PRECIS has been designed in such a way that it fulfills all these objectives successfully. It endeavours to satisfy the critics of chain indexing to a great extent.

The PRECIS is based on two principles; viz., principle of context dependency, and principle of one-to-one relationship.

PRINCIPLE OF CONTEXT DEPENDENCY

This can be best demonstrated through following examples: Indexing of documents in the library of Vidyasagar

University at Midnapore.

If the components term are organized in accordance with the Principle of context dependency then the following entries is aimed at:

Midnapore - Vidyasagar University - Library - Document -Indexing

In the above string of terms, each of the terms set the next terms into its most obvious wider context (general to specific). In this example, 'Midnapore' sets all the following concepts into their geographical context in which 'Vidyasagar University' is the locator and the "Library" is its part. "Documents" are with in the library to which indexing is done. It means that each term in the string sets the next terms into its wider context.

PRINCIPLE OF ONE-TO-ONE RELATIONSHIP

When terms are organized in context dependent order, they form a one-to-one related sequence. This simply means that each of the terms in the string is directly related to its next term. Thus, these two characteristics are the basis on which the whole system work and they play a very important role in covering the meaning of an index entry.

PRECIS is based on the codes and role operators, which form the syntactical backbone of PRECIS and regulate the writing of input string.

ROLE OPERATOR

A set of notations which specifies the grammatical role or function of the term which follows the operators and which regulates the order of the term in an input string. There are two kinds of Role Operators : Primary Operators (earlier called Main line operators) and Secondary Operators (earlier called Interposed operators). One of these operators has to be written as a prefix to each of the terms in an input string.

(A) Primary operators : It controls the sequence of terms in the input string and also determines the format of entries in the printed index. Primary operators consist of numbers in the range of 0 to 6 having built in filing value. Certain conditions must be satisfied while writing the input string. These conditions are: Every string must begin with a concept coded with an operator in the range 0 to 2, and Every string must contain a concept which is prefixed by the operator (1) and/or (2).

(B) Secondary operators: It can be introduced into a string at any point to raise its level of exhaustivity, but these operators cannot be used **to** start **a** string. Any of the secondary operators is always to be preceded by a primary operator to which it relates.

Codes : An important feature of the revised version of PRECIS is the provision of codes for bringing expresiveness in the resulting index entries. The three types of codes are - Primary, Secondary, and Typographic Codes.

PRIMARY OPERATORS

Environment of Core Concepts	0	Location
Core Concepts	1	Key system Thing when action not present Thing towards which an action is directed e.g. object of transitive action, performer of intransitive action.
	2	Action; Effect of Action
	3	Performer of transitive action (agent instrument); intake; factor
Extra-core Concepts	4	Viewpoint - as - form
	5	Selected instance; study region, study example, sample population
	6	Form of document; target user
Secondary operators		
Co-ordinate Concepts	f	'Bound' co-ordinate concept
	g	Standard – ordinate concept
Dependent Elements	p	Part; Property
	q	Member of quasi-generic group
	r	Assembly

Special Classes of Action	S Role definer; Directional property
	t Author-attributed action
	u Two-way interaction
Codes	
(a) Primary Codes	\$x 1st concept in co-ordinate theme
Theme interlinks	\$y 2nd/ subsequent concept on coordinate theme
	\$z Common concept
Term Codes	\$a Common noun
	\$c Proper Noun (Class of one)
	\$d Place name
(b) Secondary Codes	
Differences	
Preceding differences	1st and 2nd Characters :
(3 characters)	\$0 Non-lead, space generating
	\$1 Non-lead, close up
	\$2 Lead, space generating
	\$3 Lead, Close up
	3rd Character = number in the range 1-9 indicating level of difference
Date as a difference	\$d
	\$n Non-lead parenthetical difference
Parenthetical Difference	\$o Lead parenthetical difference
connectives	\$v Downward-reading connective
	\$w Upward reading connective
(c) Typographic codes	
\$e	Non filing part in italic preceded by comma
\$f	Filing part in italic preceded by comma
\$g	Filing part in roman, no preceding punctuation
\$h	Filing part in italic preceded by full point
\$i	Filing part in italic, no preceding punctuation

PREPARATION OF INPUT STRING

Two line three part entry structure is followed in PRECIS, which represents a string of five terms in one to one related sequence. A-B-C-D- E. The term A and E can act as a entry point.

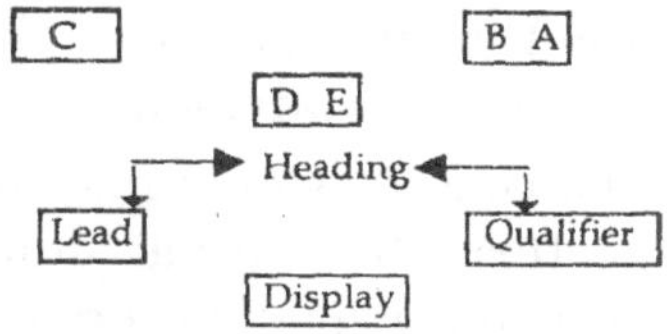

Lead : Lead *is* occupied by approach term or filing term and is offered as the user's access point in the index.

Qualifier : This position is occupied by the term(s) that sets the lead into its wider context (i.e., general to specific)

Lead and Qualifier together called 'Heading' when lead is occupied by the first term of the input string; the qualifier position is usually kept blank.

Display : This position is occupied by those terms, which rely upon the heading for their context. Sometimes, the display position becomes empty. When lead is occupied by the last term of the input string.

Example

Unemployment of skilled persons in manufacturing industries in Liverpool.

Liverpool

Manufacturing industries. Skilled persons, unemployment

Manufacturing Industries   Liverpool

Skilled Persons, Unemployment

Skilled Persons   M.I.; Liverpool

Unemployment

Unemployment   Skilled Persons Manufacturing Industries

Liverpool

APPLICATION OF PRECIS

Let us observe the application of PRECIS in the following example.

Planning of Information centre for Petrochemical Projects at Haldia.

1. Analysis of the thought content of the document and formulating its subject statement in natural language:
2. Identifying the concept signifying an action (if there be any). The term "Planning" denotes the action concept and this term should therefore be prefixed by the operator (2).
3. Identifying the kind of action represented by this term i.e., whether transitive action or intransitive action. Planning is clearly a transitive action, since it is capable of taking an object and it is coded by the operator(l). In the present example. It is the "information centre" which is being planned so the input string should now clear in the form.

   (i) Information Centres

   (ii) Planning
4. Identifying the concept, if any, related as whole-to-part. Here "Information Centre" is the part of "Petrochemical project" with the operator (1) and " information Centres" with (P). As a result we will get the following input string.

   (1) Petrochemical Projects

   (P) Information Centres

   (2) Planning
5. The remaining term "Haldia" signifies the environment (i.e., geographical location) in which the whole things take place. Accordingly the operator (o) is to be prefix to this concept and the resulting input string will be:

   (0) Haldia

   (1) Petrochemical Projects

(p) Information Centres

(2) Planning

Now *Generation of Index entries* with standard format by shunting operations.

HALDIA

Petrochemical Projects, Information Centres, Planning

Petrochemical Projects, Haldia

Information Centres, **Planning**

Information Centres, Petrochemical Projects, Haldia

Planning

Planning, Information Centres, Petrochemical Projects, Haldia

It can now be seen in the above example that lead and qualifier are separated by full stop and two spaces. The standard separator between two terms in the entry is full stop and space.

We can enhance the complexity of this subject by introducing extra dependent elements of various points in the string For the sake of demonstration we would specify that this subject had been consider in relation to India.

(0) India

(P) Haldia

(1) Petrochemical Projects

(p) Information Centres

(2) Planning

From the above discussion, it is clear that PRECIS gives a fully pre- coordinate index and is capable of producing meaningful entries from machine held files, since string formulation in PRECIS is not dependent on any classification scheme. PRECIS has also got over the problem of disappearing chains, as its keys the context intact in every entry. It is supposed to be free from all limitations which chain Procedure suffers. PRECIS may not be the best indexing system but it is believed to be a better one.

REFERENCES

1. Guha, B. *Documentation and Information: services techniques and systems, Calcutta: World, 1983.*
2. Khan, M.T.M. *Information, Organization and Communication, New Delhi: ESS ESS, 1997-98.*
3. Khanna,J.K. *Communicating Knowledge, Delhi: Research, 1996.*
4. Prasher, R.G. *Index and Indexing system, New Delhi: Medallion, 1989.*
5. Ramkrishnan, M.N. *Indexing system and Techniques, Trivendrum: Lakshmisrce, 1986.*
6. Verma, A.K. *Trends in Subject Indexing, Delhi: Mittal, 1984.*

12

Postulate Based Permuted Subject Indexing (POPSI)

The chain procedure definitely makes a period in the history of indexing, the period in which the formulation of subject in a large way was first systematized. Chain indexing enriched the world of subject indexing, not only adding new force to it but also extending its range and scope. But its fate was found with the classification schemes. In fact, the inherent weakness of the system, precisely the problem of disappearing chain and its links with the classification schemes, came to the fore and brought it less near to real life. The growth and progress of the modern age aspiring after excellence drove the stalwarts to set a new trail ablaze with live ideas which culminated in the development of new systems like POPSI in India and PRECIS in U.K.

POPSI stands for Postulate based Permuted Subject Indexing, propounded by G. Bhattacharyya. POPSI has its roots in Ranganathan's principles and postulates of the general theory of classification. It is believed that POPSI is an improved version of chain indexing. He defined POPSI in terms of its characteristics. He writes that POPSI is: An indexing system which has its primary aim to generate in the verbal plane an organizing classification (systematic grouping by Juxtaposition of a subject proposition) on the basis of a coherent set of postulates about the semantic elementary and syntactic structures of subject; and To generate on the basis of this organizing classification an associative classification by using the technique of cyclic permutation of sought terms occurring in the modulated subject propositions.

CHARACTERISTICS OF POPSI

It has the following main characteristics

1. POPSI does not recognize any absolute organizing classification.
2. It is not dependent on class numbers for deriving the chain of structured subject formulation.
3. The chain consists of elements of concepts, which occur as a part of the compound subject.
4. These elements of concepts are formulated with the help of postulates of fundamental categories, round and levels.

It is therefore, clear that although POPSI does not depend upon class numbers, yet its base is classificatory.

STEPS INVOLVED IN POPSI

The following are the main steps in the application of POPSI:

Step 1: Verbal Representation

Derivation of the postulate based verbal subject representation. It means that the subject representation is to be guided by the accepted postulates and principles. The actual work can be demonstrated with the help of an example) If the specific subject of a document to be indexed is" Oral streptomycin treatment of human lung tuberculosis: an evaluation of undesirable effects", then it is to be treated as follows:

After determining the component ideas in the subject,

linking up these ideas into sub-structures, putting the components in a helpful sequence within each sub-structure, arranging the sub-structures in a helpful sequence. The subject can be represented as:

Medicine, Human Body > Respiratory System >
Lung: [Disease - Bacteria > Mycobacterium >
Mycobacterium tuberculosis] = Tuberculosis:
Treatment – Drug > Antibiotics > Streptomycin –
Route of administration > oral; Effects >
Side effects > undesirable effects: Evaluation.

Step 2: Display of Components

Here, we consider display in a bibliographical tool, such as catalogue. Hence the display has to be linear.

Step 3: Short Display

The full representation prepared in Step 1 can now be reduced for the user into the following name of subjects:

Medicine, Lung: Tuberculosis: Treatment

Streptomycin - Oral administration; undesirable effects: Evaluation.

Step 4: Approach Terms

Using the full representation of the subject select all components and alternatives terms for the compounds, which may be used for finding information about the subject.

Step 5: Subject Index Entries

Subject index entries are to be derived from the full subject representation such that each of the approach terms selected occurs as head terms of the entries.

Step 6: Display of Subject Index Entries

A preferred method of display of the subject index entry may consist of three sections:

Section 1 Head term section

Section 2 Subject Representation Section

Section 3 Reference Section

Some of the subject index entries will be as follows:

Evaluation, Undesirable Effects

Medicine, Lung; Tuberculosis: Treatment

Streptomycin - oral; undesirable effects: Evaluation

Lung Medicine

Medicine, Lung; Tuberculosis: Treatment

Streptomycin - oral; undesirable effects: Evaluation

Drug, Treatment, Tuberculosis

Medicine, Lung; Tuberculosis: Treatment

Streptomycin - oral; undesirable effects: Evaluation

Step 7: Cross Reference

Cross Reference Index Entries (see references) are to be prepared for each of the alternatives, near-synonyumous and synonymous terms for the component terms in the subject representation.

Therapautics *see* Treatment

Therapy *see* Treatment

Cross Reference Entries *(see also* references) are to be prepared for each closely related or collateral idea or subject. For example:

Streptopenicillin *see also* Streptomycin.

Streptomycin *see also* Streptopenicillin

Step 8: Alphabetical Arrangement

The subject index entries, subject cross reference entries, and subject cross reference index entries, prepared according to the above procedure, are to be merged and arranged in a single alphabetical sequence.

MODERN VERSION OF POPSI

Bhattacharya gave a new version of POPSI: The most

important feature of the new version is that a new set of elementary categories has been recommended. They are:

D Discipline

E Entity

A Action

P Property

M Modifier

They have been explained as follows:

Discipline : An elementary category that includes conventional fields of study, or any aggregate of such fields; e.g. physical sciences, physics, chemistry etc.

Entity : An elementary category that includes manifestation having perceptual correlates, or only conceptual existence, as contrasted with their properties, and actions performed by them or on them; e.g. Energy, Light, Plants, Animals, Place, Time, Environment etc.

Action : An elementary category that includes manifestations denoting the concept of 'doing'. Action may manifest as self-Action, or External Action, e.g. Function, Migration, Selection, Organization, Evaluation etc.

Property : An elementary category that includes manifestations denoting the concept of 'attribute' - qualitative, or quantitative; e.g. property, effect, power, capability, efficiency, utility, form etc.

Modifier : In relation to a manifestation of any one of the elementary categories D,E,A and P, the term 'modifier' refers to an idea used or intended to be used to qualify the manifestation without disturbing the conceptual wholeness of the latter, e.g. "Infections" in "Infectious diseases". Any manifestation of any elementary category may serve as the basis for deriving a Modifier.

STAGES OF OPERATION

The index entries according to this system are arranged in a systematic manner with the help of following steps of operation:

(i) Analysis of the Subject Indicative Expression

(ii) Formalization of the Subject-proposition

(iii) Standardization of the subject-proposition

(iv) Modulation of the subject-proposition

(v) Preparation of Entry for Organizing Classification (EOC)

(vi) Decision about Terms of Approach (TA)

(vii) Preparation of Entries for Associative Classification (EAC)

(viii) Alphabetization

Let us examine these stages with the help of an example, i.e., "Chemical treatment of tuberculosis of lungs".

(i) Analysis : Subject Indicative Expression, the starting point for index generation, may be a title of a paper, a book or any other document. According to the first stage of operation, this expression is analyzed to identify the facets in terms of concepts and modifiers. Analysis of the above mentioned example will led to the followings:

Medicine (D)

Chemical Treatment (A)

Tuberculosis (P)

Lungs (E)

Out of these four expressions, only the first one is implicit and all the rest are explicit by nature.

(ii) Formalization : In the stage of formalization the sequence of components derived by analysis has to be decided. The accepted sequence of the system is D, E, A modified or unmodified, appropriately interpolated or extrapolated by P, modified or unmodified. Applying this principle, the components are sequenced in the following manner to obtain the basic chain:

Medicine (D), Lungs (E), Tuberculosis (P of E), Chemical treatment (A on P).

(iii) Standardization : The third stage in concerned with the semantics of POPSI language. This step of standardization helps to decide the standard terms for synonyms and the terms for reference generation. In the present example, 'chemical treatment' may be substituted by 'chemotherapy' as a result of this operation for standardization. A vocabulary control mechanism is used to achieve this goal. This operation results in the standardized basic chain like the following:

Medicine (D), Lungs (E), Tuberculosis (P of E), Chemotherapy (=chemical treatment) (A on P).

(iv) Modulation : The fourth stage of operation augments the standardized subject formulation by interpolating or extrapolating the successive super ordinates by using standard terms along with their synonyms. This step also involves semantic aspect of POPSI as vocabulary control is necessary here. On applying this operation, we get the basic modulated chain.

Medicine (D), Man, Respiratory System, Lungs (E), Disease.

Tuberculosis (P of E), Treatment. Chemotherapy (=chemical treatment) (A on P)

(v) Preparation of EOC : This step leads to the preparation of the main entry, which is further used for generation of associative entries. In order to achieve this goal, a systematic set of numbers as given in the POPSI table is used to indicate the categories and positions of the components in the subject formulation.

0	Form modifier
1	General treatment
2	Phase relation
2.1	General
2.2	Bias
2.3	Comparison
2.4	Similarity

2.5	Difference
2.6	Application
2.7	Influence
	Common Modifier
3	Time Modifier
4	Environment Modifier
5	Phase Modifier

6	Entity	Action	Part
7	Discipline	Property	species type special modifier
	Preceded by the number Of the manifestation in Relation to which it is Action/ Property		
8	Core	Features analogous to 6 Entity/ 7 Discipline	
9	Base		

POPSI Table

The structure of the entry after this operation will be shaped in the following fashion:

Medicine 6, Man, Respiratory system, Lungs 6.2 Disease.

Tuberculosis 6.2.1 Treatment. Chemotherapy.

A notation for manifestation of Discipline (D) is omitted in the basic version of POPSI. Decreasing ordinal value of category numbers is followed in sequencing of components.

(vi) Decision about TA : This step is concerned with the decision regarding terms of approach for generating successive index entries and references. In this process of selection, generalized terms like man, animal etc. and common terms like efficiency; evaluation is omitted from entry points. During this operation synonyms are controlled and references are generated from synonyms to standard terms. In the present example, 'chemotherapy' has been accepted in the vocabulary in place of 'chemical treatment'. Accordingly, the following reference is genera ted

Chemical treatment

See chemotherapy

In this example all the terms other than 'Medicine' and 'Man' are selected as approach terms.

(vi) Preparation of EAC : This step arranges entries under each approach terms. The complete subject formulation is repeated under all the approach terms from the index phrase. Thus for the present example one of the entries will be

Respiratory System

Medicine 6 Man, Respiratory system, Lungs 6.2

Disease. Tuberculosis 6.2.1 Treatment

Chemotherapy.

Similar entries will be generated under other approach terms - Lungs, Disease, Tuberculosis, Treatment and Chemotherapy.

(viii) Alphabetization : Here, all the index entries including references are arranged in a word-by-word sequence. The final display of index entries generated from the cited example is shown in the following manner:

Chemical treatment

See Chemotherapy

Chemotherapy

Medicine 6 Man, Respiratory system, Lungs 6.2 Disease.

Tuberculosis 6.2.1 Treatment. Chemotherapy.

Disease

Medicine 6 Man, Respiratory system, Lungs 6.2 Disease.

Tuberculosis 6.2.1 Treatment. Chemotherapy.

Lungs

Medicine 6 Man, Respiratory system, Lungs 6.2

Disease.

Tuberculosis 6.2.1 Treatment. Chemotherapy.

Respiratory System

Medicine 6 Man, Respiratory system, Lungs 6.2 Disease.

Tuberculosis 6.2.1 Treatment. Chemotherapy.

Therapy

Medicine 6 Man, Respiratory system, Lungs 6.2 Disease.

Tuberculosis 6.2.1 Treatment. Chemotherapy.

Treatment

Medicine 6 Man, Respiratory system, Lungs 6.2 Disease.

Tuberculosis 6.2.1 Treatment. Chemotherapy.

Tuberculosis

Medicine 6 Man, Respiratory system, Lungs 6.2 Disease.

Tuberculosis 6.2.1 Treatment. Chemotherapy.

ADVANTAGES OF POPSI

POPSI is helpful in

1. Formulating subject headings, which may be used as feature heading or for other indexing purposes.
2. Deriving subject index entries for a classified catalogue, an index to a book etc.
3. Determining the subject of readers query in a consistent and helpful way.
4. Formulating a strategy for searching information about a subject in a catalogue or other surrogate files,and
5. Deriving a base for the presentation of ideas in the text of a document.

POPSI, it may have been observed, is not based upon any scheme of classification but uses ideas and theory of classification both in the analysis of subjects and also in the structuring of the names of subjects. In fact, POPSI can be used for various purposes. POPSI has introduced the use of indicator digits, in the full representation of subjects, as an additional syntactical device. POPSI has also introduced a better format and method of display of entries.

REFERENCES

1. Ghosh, S.B. and Satpathi, J.N. ed. *Subject indexing systems concepts methods and techniques. Calcutta: IASLIC, 1998.*
2. Guha, B. *Documentation and Information; services techniques and systems. Calcutta: World, 1983.*
3. Khan, M.T.M. *Information, Organization and Communication, New Delhi: ESS ESS, 1997-98.*
4. Khanna, J.K., *Communicating Knowledge, Delhi: Research.*
5. Prasher, R.G. *Index and Indexing system, New Delhi: Medallion, 1989.*
6. Ramkrishnan, M.N. *Indexing system and Techniques, Trivendrum:* Lakshmisree, 1986.

13

Keyword Indexing

The idea of keyword indexing technique to represent subject matter of documents is not new. There are evidences of its use in the 19th century, when it was referred to as catchword indexing Andrea Crestadoro introduced it as early as 1856 under the name 'keyword in titles' for the catalogue of the Manchester Public Library. He also included it in his author catalogue of 1864 as a 'concordance of titles' to provide a quasi-subject approach. The keyword indexing technique has also been used for many years in bibliographical tools such as "British Books in Print".

BASIC PRINCIPLE

Keyword indexing is based on the improved methodology of its production i.e. by computer, and also in its physical layout of display rather than principle. 'Keyword' means catchword or significant word mainly taken from the title and/ or sometimes from abstract or text of a document for the purpose of generation of indexes. Thus, keyword indexing is based on the natural language of the document to get index entries and no controlled vocabulary is normally required for this indexing system. Here, entries are made under each keyword selected from the purpose. The words chosen may be single words, multi words or even phrases that convey the content. Several keywords may be chosen for a document to provide access to different user requirements. This principle has been applied in the modern keyword indexing system and its variations. Even with a slight variation, it has taken different names though the principle remains the same.

KWIC (KEYWORD-IN-CONTEXT)

H.P. Luhn tried to exploit potentialities of computer to derive a solution to the problem of speedy dissemination of information. He and his associates produced and distributed copies of machine produced title index in the international conference of scientific information at Washington in 1958. Luhn named his index keyword-in-context index (KWIC) and reported the method of generation of such an index in a paper in 1959. The value of KWIC was established with its adoption by the American Chemical Society in 1960 in its publication 'Chemical Titles'.

The KWIC method of indexing rests on the presumption:

(i) That the title of a document fully expresses the subject of the document,

(ii) The subject can be indicated reasonably accurately with the help of the key terms used in the title;

(iii) In case of an entry under one term the context or the subject background indicated by the other terms need not be stated in any organized order; and

(iv) The entry term along with the full title or even a part of it that can be accommodated within the printing space available, will enable the user to guess whether the document will be of interest to him or not.

FORMAT AND STRUCTURE

Each entry in KWIC index consists of three parts: keywords, context and identification or location code.

(a) Keywords : Significant words of the title, which serve as approach/ access terms.

(b) Context : The rest of the terms of the title along with the keywords specify the context of the document.

(c) Identification or Location Code : A code, which provides address of the document where its full bibliographic description will be available.

The format of KWIC can be explained with the help of an example. Take a document with identification code 1279 entitled 'Classification of Books in a University Library'. This will have the following entries according to KWIC indexing system:

BOOKS in a University Library/ Classification of	1279
CLASSIFICATION of Books in a University Library	1279
LIBRARY / Classification of Books in a University	1279
UNIVERSITY Library/ Classification of Books in a	1279

The first word in each entry - Books, Classification, Library and University is a keyword. The part of the title following each keyword is the context. The number attached with each entry on the extreme right is the identification number. The keyword can be at the extreme left as shown above, and it may also be in the centre as given below:

Classification of BOOKS in a University Library	1279
University Library/ CLASSIFICATION of Books in a	1279
in a University LIBRARY / Classification of Books	1279
of Books in a UNIVERSITY Library / Classification	1279

Thus, the significant words, or keywords, are selected from the title. These are used as access points to the search or as approach terms by turn. In each entry, the remaining part of the title serves, as the context on the extreme right of each entry there is an Identification Number, which indicates the location of the document. Each entry is then filed at an appropriate place in the alphabetical sequence of the index file.

OPERATIONAL STAGES IN KWIC INDEXING

(a) The keywords are selected from the title and / or abstract and / or text of the document.

(b) The significant words (in case of computerized system) marked as stop list is prepared and kept in the computer. The 'stop list' is 'stop words' or words on a 'kill list', which are considered to have no value for indexing and no index entries, will be produced for the terms included in the list. These include insignificant words such as articles (a, an, the), prepositions, conjunctions, pronouns, auxiliary verbs together with such general words as 'aspect', 'very', 'different' etc. The larger the list, the fewer the index entries one would expect. Each major search system has defined their own 'stop words' list indiscriminate marking of article, prepositions etc. may create problems of retrieval in many cases because of important scientific and technical terms such as 'Vitamin A', 'on-line' etc. which have significant meaning.

(c) The index is generated under significant terms by placing it at the appropriate position (usually in the middle) and other words in the title are wrapped around it, which serve as a context.

(d) The last word and first word of the title are separated by using a symbol (/) or other symbols (sometimes an asterisk '*' is used).

(e) The identification / location codes are printed at the right end of the each entry.

(f) The index entries are arranged alphabetically by keywords.

Let us take the title 'control of damages of rice by insects' to demonstrate the index entries generated through KWIC principle.

CONTROL of damages of rice by insects	118
DAMAGES of rice by insects/control of	118
INSECTS/ Control of damages of rice by	118
RICE by insects / control of damages of	118

Here, the filing keywords are placed in the left side of the page.

VARIATIONS OF KEYWORD INDEX

Although the basic concept of KWIC indexing system remains unchanged since its introduction, yet its physical form and intellectual contents have undergone some changes, Examples are:

KWOC (KEYWORD-OUT-OF-CONTEXT)

The KWOC is a variant of KWIC index. Here, each keyword is taken out of the title and printed separately in the left hand margin with the complete title printed along with it. This gives the advantages of having a familiar appearance of filing words at the left and also presenting the whole title as it exists.

Example:

Control	Control of damages of rice by insects	118
Damages	Control of damages of rice by insects	118
Insects	Control of damages of rice by insects	118
Rice	Control of damages of rice by insects	118

KEYWORD-AWAY FROM THE CONTEXT

In this, keywords are printed as headings and the titles are printed in the next line instead of the same line.

Example:

Control	Control of damages of rice by insects	118
Damages	Control of damages of rice by insects	118
Rice	Control of damages of rice by insects	118
Insects	Control of damages of rice by insects	118

KWAC (KEYWORD-AUGMENTED-IN-CONTEXT)

KWAC also stands for 'Keyword And Context'. In many cases, titles can not always represent the thought content of the document co- extensively. KWIC and KWOC could not solve the problem of retrieval of irrelevant documents. To solve the problem of false retrieval, KWAC provided the methodology of enrichment of the keywords of the title with additional keywords taken either from the abstract or from the original documents text and then inserted into the title or added at the end to give further index entries. The CBAC (Chemical Biological Activities) or B1OS1S uses KWAC index, where the titles are indexed by other words taken from the abstract or text.

KWWC (KEYWORD-WITH-CONTEXT)

Here the full title (i.e. context) is not repeated with every keyword in the entry. Only that part of the title, which is considered relevant to the keyword, is provided in the entry. Sometimes, for the purpose of bringing expressiveness in the index entries, a secondary aspect or the scope of the subject is added to the primary aspect, separated by a punctuation mark The example of KWWC index is given below with the help of the title "Bacterial contamination in Indian distilleries using waste molasses as raw materials".

Alcohol fermentation / Effect of bacterial contamination

Bacterial Contamination / Effect on alcohol fermentation

Fermentation, alcoholic / Effect of bacterial contamination

Molasses / alcohol fermentation; Effect of bacterial contamination

KEYTALPHA (KEY-TERM ALPHABETICAL) INDEX

It is a permuted subject index that lists only keywords assigned to each abstract. Here, keywords are arranged side by side. Eliminating the insignificant words, without forming a sentence.

The index entries for a document entitled 'control of rice by insects' will be as follows :

CONTROL, Damages, Rice, Insects	118
DAMAGES, Rice, Insects. Control	118
INSECTS, Control, Damages, Rice	118
RICE, Insects, Control, Damages	118

KEYTALPHA index has been used in the 'oceanic abstracts'

WADEX (WORD AND AUTHOR INDEX)

An improved variation of KWIC index is WADEX where the names of authors are also treated as keywords in addition to the significant subject terms, thus, facilitating and satisfying author approach of the document also. It is used in' Applied Mechanics Review'; AKWIC (Author- and-Keyword-in-context) index is another version of WADEX.

DOUBLE KWIC INDEX

This is another improved version of KWIC index, involving two- stage operation i.e., Each keyword extracted from the title is considered as entry word and is used as heading; and Under each entry word, titles are rotated in such a way that each keyword comes in the beginning as the approach term, by rotation, folJowed by the rest of the title. The entry word is eliminated from the title and is replaced by a '.' sign. Other signs (either '/' or '-' or '@') may also be used to denote the end of a title. Here, index entries are arranged alphabetically by the entry words and under each entry word, rotated titles are arranged alphabetically.

KLIC (KEY-LETTER-IN-CONTEXT)

Here, complete words are not selected for indexing. This system allows truncation of words, either at the beginning (i.e. left truncation) where a fragment (i.e. key letters) can be specified and the computer may pick up any term containing that fragment.

The chemical society (London) published a KLIC index as a guide to truncations.

COLUMNAR KWIC

In keyword indexing, entries are made under single term or phrase in a single central column. In columnar KWIC, entries are presented in a number of recognizable columns shown horizontally and they represent the attributes of the subject. Here, straight-forward titles may not be used.

ONLINE KWIC

Because of the availability of large scale commercial online information retrieval services and increasing availability of computer facilities in the form of online terminals, experiments are being made for cheaper, easier, and user-friendly systems for subject approach to such commercial databases. One such experiment is online KWIC index in which searches are carried out covering a number of commercial databases. Here, the online KWIC program cumulates the subject indexes of different databases into a single unified KWIC index and a user searches desired items from different databases through a regular online search. This may better be termed as 'Cumulated KWIC.

USES OF KEYWORD INDEXES

A number of indexing and abstracting services produce their subject indexes by using variations of keyword indexing techniques. Some notable examples are:

(a) Chemical Titles

(b) Basic (Biological Abstracts subject in context)

(c) Keyword Index of Chemical Abstracts

(d) Index of Conference proceedings Received - a monthly list of the proceedings received by the BLLD.

(e) CBAC (Chemical Biological Activities)

MERITS OF KEYWORD INDEXING

1. The principal merit of keyword indexing is the speed with which it can be produced.

2. The production of keyword index does not involve intellectual effort and thus it saves costly efforts of indexing staff. What is required is an expressive title co-extensive with the subject of the document.
3. Vocabulary control is not required.
4. Satisfies the current approaches of information of users, as it facilitates production of current awareness services.
5. Works very well for specific subject/ aspect search.

DEMERITS OF KEYWORD INDEXING

1. The efficiency of keyword indexing depends invariably on the question of reliability of expressive titles of documents, as most of such indexes are based on titles. If the titles are not meaningful, the system becomes ineffective, particularly in humanities and social sciences.
2. Most of the terms used in science and technology are standardized so the problem of natural language vocabulary is not so acute. But the situation is different in case of humanities and social sciences where consistency in usage of terms is not there.
3. Related topics are scattered. Search for a topic may have to be made under several keywords. As a result, search time may be high in many circumstances.
4. Searches very often lead to high recall and low precision.
5. It fails to meet the exhaustive approach to information from a large collection.

The keyword index has been quite popular during the last five decades. A number of evaluation studies have indicated that keyword indexing may offer several advantages over other conventional systems. The continued growth of machine-readable databases has shown that the use of keyword indexes works well in information retrieval.

The problem of inexpensive title is solved to a considerable extent by editorial intervention, which means that more time will be required for its production. In the preparation of current awareness type of lists, this indexing appears to be more effective in terms of time, effort and cost. Even an individual library or information centre may use keyword index for its in-house publications.

It is true that this indexing system is not able to meet the requirements of exhaustive literature search and thereby is unable to totally replace other conventional systems. But it has proved to be most successful in the field of current awareness services.

REFERENCES

1. Ghosh, S.B. and Satpathi. *Subject Indexing Systems: Concepts, Methods and Techniques. Calcutta: IASLIC, 1998.*
2. Khanna, Dr. J.K. *Communicating Knowledge. Kurukshetra: Research Publications, 1999.*
3. Prasher, R.G. *Index and Indexing Systems, New Delhi: Medallion Press, 1989.*
4. Verma, A.K. *Trend in Subject indexing. Delhi: Mittal, 1984.*

14

Cyclic Indexing

Cyclic indexing is a pre-coordinate indexing and a pre-coordinate indexing system is that in which terms are combined or coordinated at the time of indexing by the indexer. In pre-coordinate systems, documents are searched under the same terms which the indexer originally assigned to them without any further manipulation of terms at the time of searching.

PRE - COORDINATE SYSTEMS

- Permutation Indexes
  - Rotated indexing
  - Cyclic indexing
  - SLIC indexing (selective listing in combination)
- Fixed Citation order
  - Articulated subject Indexing
  - Chain indexing
  - PRECIS, NEPHIS
  - systematic indexing
- General
  - Subject card index to library Catalogues
  - Book or periodical Subject indexes
  - other printed indexes.

Two issues recur in all pre-coordinate indexes :

1. The first issue is concerned with the consistent description of subjects with many concept headings. Consistency must be instilled both in the terms used

to describe the individual concepts that comprise the multi concept heading and also into the order in which those individual concept terms are cited or listed.

2. The second issue concerns to provide access for those users who approach the subject under consideration for indexing from one of the 'secondary concepts'. Only one term can appear in the primary position in the prescribed citation order. The preferred citation order should be that which is believed to match the approach of many users. References or added entries must supplement the first or main entry and cater for access from other angles.

The above two issues are applicable to cyclic indexing as well.

CONCEPT OF CYCLIC INDEXING

To approach a composite heading via one of the concepts that does not take the first position in the citation order, access to secondary concepts is provided. This system relies upon moving the index term in the heading through the various positions in the heading. While using the computer for creating a series of headings from index string, it is desired that there should be some algorithm for the generation of references and added entries.

Therefore cyclic indexing involves the movement of the first lead term to the last position in the subsequent entry. This process is repeated until each concept has occupied the lead position.

To illustrate this symbolically, we can take a composite subject represented by 5 notational symbols ABCDE, representing the words abcde.

ABCDE = 5 notational symbols

abcde = words represented by notational symbols ABCDE, where-

a = Law represented by A

b = Corruption represented by B

c = Bureaucracy represented by C

d = Pakistan represented by D

e = Checking represented by E

One place entry means one entry at ABCDE and 5 index entries:

edcba	(see)	ABCDE
dcba	(see)	ABCD
cba	(see)	ABC
ba	(see)	AB
a	(see)	A

Cycling involves 5 entries and also 5 index entries, but this time the index entries are for the individual elements only not for any composite subjects.

Entries	index entries
ABCDE	a (see) A
BCDEA	b (see) B
CDEAB	c (see) C
DEABC	d (see) D
EABCD	e (see) E

Example

ABCDE Law: Corruption: Bureaucracy: Pakistan: Checking BCDEA Corruption: Bureaucracy: Pakistan: Checking: Law CDEAB Bureaucracy: Pakistan: Checking: Law: Corruption DEABC Pakistan: Checking: Law: Corruption: Bureaucracy EABCD Checking: Law: Corruption: Bureaucracy: Pakistan

(i) Cycling is frequently used with UDC, where numbers may be combined by using the colon:

(ii) When only 2 numbers are concerned the cycled entry is simple. The reverse of the primary entry and the technique is often known as reversing.

Several indexers have suggested/modifications to the cyclic indexing method for a multiple entry system prescribed by the guide to UDC (BC 1000 C: 1963) cyclic indexing as conventionally used in multiple entry classified catalogue is a rotated A/Z index agreed with the standard citation order. It may also be used with certain modifications in a single entry system. ,

Due to interdisciplinary nature of research, subject indexing became a complicated process. Since most of the documents of present day cover composite subjects, representation of subject with a single index term looked impossible and it called for a combination or coordination of a number of terms. Cyclic indexing is one of the methods that help in representation of subject in more precise manner and increases specificity of index and search.

REFERENCES

1. Riaz, Muhammad, *Modern Techniques of Document and Information work. Delhi: Royal, 1992.*
2. Verma, A.K., *Trends in subject indexing. Delhi: Mittal, 1984.*

15

Indexing Languages

Language plays a vital role in indexing. Any language that is used for indexing may be called an indexing language. In that sense even a natural language when used in indexing may be called an indexing language. But technically an indexing language is often differentiated from a natural language in the sense that any language or a system has its own ingredients. One of such ingredient is "the element of vocabulary which comprises of sounds (physical sound or written marks) used to designate the physical objects or mental constructs they refer to (referents).

NATURAL LANGUAGE AND ITS PROBLEMS

A natural language is one, which people use, in their day-to-day communication both spoken and written. A natural language has a good vocabulary and has the flexibility of incorporating of new terms. It also has syntax to represent correct association of terms. But its use in indexing may not be so effective. The problems of using natural language in indexing are described below:

(1) A concept may be represented by different terms e.g. the concept "house" may be specified not only by the term house but also other terms such as " abode" and "dwelling". This manifests the richness of the language

but if all these terms are used in an index, the document dealing with this concept will be scattered in the alphabetical file. This is the problem of synonyms.

(2) There may be words with same spelling but different meanings Game - play, thick, hunted animal.

A term when used alone, may not carry exact meaning. This is the problem of homographs.

(3) With the change of gender of noun words the spelling and even world change e.g. Dog, Bitch. This will naturally get scattered in the alphabetical order. This is the problem of gender

(4) There may be the different spelling of the same word e.g. Color, Colour; Connexion, Connection.

(5) Different word forms may be created by the use of suffixes e.g. cool, cooling, cooler, coollant. They are related concepts and will be scattered in alphabetical sequence due to difference in spelling.

The problem of natural language make it necessary to have a separate language for indexing which has power to control vocabulary, flexibility to show relation of different concepts and facility to built up a searchable file providing access to all possible access points of users.

Indexing language is generally defined as "all the words permitted either to describe a specific document or to construct a query to search a document file, along with the rules describing how the terms are to be used and in what relation to each other."

CHARACTERISTICS OF INDEXING LANGUAGE

The following characteristics of the indexing languages may be identified:

(1) The vocabulary of an indexing language has to be very precise and exact. Both synonyms and homonyms are to be avoided. In fact near synonyms are also to be avoided. As far as possible, a complete one to one correspondence between concept and terms need to be

maintained.

(2) When a number of terms have to be used in the complete subject formulation, the question of putting the terms in the most appropriate order comes. In other words some rules of syntax are necessary. As in any natural language, the rules of syntax control, the construction of a phrase, clause or sentence, so in an indexing language also some rules of syntax are necessary for correctly constructing the names of subjects. In fact in an indexing language the syntax or the order of words in a subject formulation is much more important than in a natural language.

In a natural language, apart from the substantive words, a number of other auxiliaries like preposition, conjunction etc. are also used which help to bring out the correct meaning of the substantives and also the meaning of the construction as a whole. But in an indexing language such auxiliaries are not available and hence the correct meaning of a subject or index heading has to be expressed largely through the order of words. Hence, the rule of syntax deals essentially with order of words or terms.

(3) The third characteristics of an indexing language is that, apart from the word order prescribed by its rules of syntax, it becomes necessary at times, to use relational symbols or indicator digit to bring out the correct relation between the words. Thus in class numbers, which are subject formulations in indexing language constructed according to a scheme of classification we find connecting symbols are used between component concepts. In the indexing used by the British Technology index, operators like comma (,), double comma ("), colon (:) etc. are used to show the correct relationship between words. Similarly the POPSI subject heading also includes the indicator digits for the same purpose.

(4) Due to the last two characteristics, an indexing language needs to have another mechanism. When a subject has been formulated in the preferred index language, it can provide only a single access in the searchable index file. To provide access from the other words or concepts of the many subject formulation, provision of a special mechanism or device is necessary for rotating or changing the position of the words in such a way that the correct meaning is available from such approach point. The usual mechanism available is a system of orderly rotation of terms. These rules of rotation are actually special rules of syntax in an indexing language. Relational operators mentioned earlier may also help this mechanism

TYPES OF INDEXING LANGUAGE

Indexing process involves two basic operators; i.e., Content analysis; and Processing of the content of the documents for organization of searchable file.

Therefore both are now taken to be variation of indexing language. Thus the indexing languages are of following types.

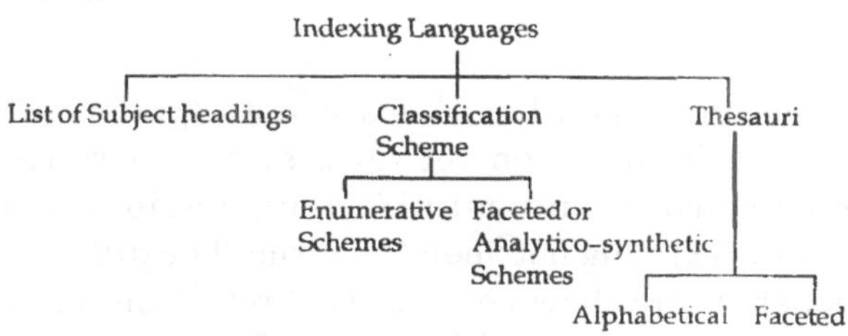

1. Standard List of Subject Headings

A subject heading list is a standard list of terms to be used as subject headings, either for the whole field of knowledge or a limited subject area including references made to and from each term, notes explaining the scope and usage of certain headings, and occasionally corresponding class numbers. Such a list is normally arranged alphabetically Both preferred and rejected terms are listed in the same sequence. The terms are linked by see and see also references. The most well known subject heading list for the whole field of knowledge are Library of Congress subject Headings and Sears List of Subject Headings, while Medical Subject Heading (MeSH) is an example of subject heading list of **a** limited subject area.

2. Classification Schemes

A classification scheme is a list of class terms with corresponding notation, accompanied by an alphabetical index. The two major types of classification schemes are - enumerative and faceted classification schemes. An enumerative scheme consists of a single list or schedule of all class terms representing a universe, while a faceted scheme consists of different schedules of class terms representing different facets of the universe. The well known enumerative and near enumerative classification schemes are 'Library of Congress Classification and 'Dewey Decimal Classification. The example of facted classification and near facted classification is Colon Classification and Universal Decimal Classification Scheme

3. Thesaurus

A thesaurus is a list of descriptors (preferred terms) for use in an information retrieval system arranged in **a** systematic order and manifesting various types of relationships existing between the terms The different types of relationships are shown by use of abbreviations or symbols. eg. UNESCO thesaurus, Thesaurus for Engineering and Scientific Term (TEST) and INIS Thesaurus.

It is interesting to note that an alphabetical language is always dependent on a natural language since the main vocabulary of such a language is borrowed from a natural language and hence for an index to be consulted by persons should be familiar with that language, but a notational indexing language, such a classification scheme is independent of any natural language.

ATTRIBUTES OF INDEXING LANGUAGE

Index is a tool for information retrieval and retrieval of information requires, the quarry analysis, matching process and the knowledge of the index as a tool (i.e. how it is used). This match is possible if the file is organized in a predetermined order and the users are aware of it. In successful organization of the file and subsequent matching of documents and requests, semantics and syntax of indexing language have very important role to play.

(a) Vocabulary Control

The vocabulary of an indexing language is controlled so that there is one to one relationship between the concepts and the terms representing them. This is done by strictly avoiding synonyms, near synonyms and homonyms. In an indexing language, where codes or symbols are used instead of terms. The basic vocabulary is often taken from a natural language but the vocabulary thus adopted may differ from the vocabulary of the original language.

(b) Concept Coordination

A subject cannot be represented by only one term. When multiple terms are used, proper representation of subject depends on correct coordination of terms. To solve this problem, some indexing languages have made provision for relational symbols, which are known as role operators, role indicators, indicator digits etc. Coordination of terms is carried out at the input stage in pre-coordinate indexing and at output stage in post-coordinate indexing.

(c) Multiple Access

When a subject representation is formulated with the help of the rules of syntax, the concepts are arranged in a linear order, which can provide only a single access in a searchable index file. To provide access from other terms indexing language provides some rules of rotation of component terms. The rotation is done in such a way that each of the component term is placed in the access position, which is followed by other terms.

(d) Syndetic Devices

Indexing language is an artificial language; it requires some syndetic devices for the guidance and assistance of the users. These are:

(i) Cross References

Cross-references such as see and see also or use and used for are used to link non-preferred and preferred term.

(ii) Glossaries

The extension of the preferred term is sometimes limited or expanded to ensure a definite coverage. Scope notes, explanation, enumerations etc indicate this.

e.g. Cell physiology (SN structural property of cells)

(iii) Inverted Headings

The normal order of words in a heading is sometimes inverted to bring the potent word in the beginning since users approach is expected by that word or to avoid scattering of related materials

eg. Bridges, Concrete

(e) Relation Manifestation

Elementary terms of every language are related to each other semantically and syntagmatically. This is true for indexing languages as well. "Semantic relations are those which are known in advance before scanning any particular document, while syntagmatic relations are understood only after scanning a particular document".

(i) Semantic Relationship

In an indexing language, semantic relations include broader -narrower relation and associated relation and those are often indicated by the arrangement of terms such as

Chemistry

Organic Chemistry

Inorganic Chemistry

Metals

This shows that Organic Chemistry and Inorganic Chemistry are . parts of Chemistry. Organic and Inorganic are of same levels and Metals is a part of Inorganic Chemistry.

(ii) Syntagmatic Relationship

Syntagmatic relation is restricted to a particular document. The relation is established between different concepts covered in the document only after the analysis of the subject content, e.g. a document entitled 'Law of inheritance and social status of women in rural India' has a combination of concepts from law, sociology and geography, which is special combination, not normally shown in any indexing language. To manifest this relation, an indexing language has to device some mechanism. A faceted classification for example, provides separate schedules of isolates for different subjects and even for different facets under each subject, and the required combination of concepts is achieved by use of indicator digits.

(f) Structural Presentation

Since indexing language aim at efficient retrieval of documents, it has to consider the characteristics of users approaches. If a user did not find information about particular subject, then he is looking for broader, narrower, collateral terms, and for such relations, there should be systematic presentation is required. This is done by different methods in different languages. In thesaurus - BT, NT are used whereas a classification scheme shows the broader, narrower relation by notation.

(g) Effectiveness

Indexing language can be checked on the basis of performance of the indexing system using that language in information retrieval. The well known evaluative method of indexing system is Precision and Recall. Higher ratio reflects higher effectiveness of the language used.

Due to entry of computers in the field of indexing, it has now been possible to use even natural languages in indexing work. In spite of their ambiguity and lack of compactness, the natural languages can hardly compete with artificial indexing languages in overall efficiency. Therefore, indexing languages will continue to play an important role in indexing work for a long time to come.

REFERENCES

1. Ghosh, S.B. and Satpathi, *J.N. Subject Indexing system: concepts, methods and techniques. Calcutta: IASLIC, 1998.*
2. Rajan, T.N. *Indexing Systems: concepts, models and techniques. Calcutta: IASLIC, 1981.*
3. Riaz, Muhammad. *Modern Techniques of Documentation and information work . Delhi:Royal, 1992.*

16

Thesaurus

The Word 'Thesaurus' comes from Greek term 'thesauros' meaning a storehouse or treasury of words. Dictionary defines it as 'a book of words or of information about a particular field or a set of concepts, specially a dictionary of synonyms'. Peter Mark Roget first constructed thesaurus in year 1852. Since then, the term thesaurus has become almost synonymous with Roget. The term thesaurus detached from Roget's name only in 1957 when Helen Brownson used the term thesaurus in the context of information retrieval. H.P. Luhn was the first person to think in terms of information retrieval thesaurus. Du Pont in USA around 1969 and developed the first thesaurus used in information retrieval system then many thesauri have been brought out in different subject field.

Thesaurus has been defined in ISO-2788 (1974) in terms of its functions and structure. In terms of function, it states, "a thesaurus is a terminological control device used in translating from the natural language of documents, indexes or users into a more constrained 'system language' (documentation language, information language)". In terms of its structure, the standard says, "a thesaurus is a controlled and dynamic vocabulary of semantically and generically related terms which cover a specific domain of knowledge"

In simple words thesaurus may be described as a compilation of descriptors for use in an information retrieval system arranged in an alphabetical order and manifesting the various types of relationships existing between the descriptors. An Information retrieval thesaurus is a kind of semantic networking of concepts.

FUNCTIONS OF A THESAURUS

Thesaurus provides a standard vocabulary for a given subject field by exercising control on a vocabulary of terms used in an indexing language. Controlling the vocabulary is done by the following methods; out of all the possible synonyms and quasi-synonyms, only one terms is selected as a descriptor; the scope of the meaning of the term is clearly indicated in a scope note for the best suitability of the selected meaning; a definite rule is followed for compound terms, word-forms, number (singular, plural) and spellings are standardized; and homonyms are differentiated by qualifiers.

Apart from the above functions thesaurus shows the intrinsic, semantic relationship existing between terms and thus provides system of references between terms. It helps the indexer and the searcher in the choice of preferred terms. It provides hierarchical display of terms so that a search can be broadened or narrowed systematically. It increases the speed of retrieval by use of indexing terms and search terms and It provides a map of a given subject field, which help to understand the structure of the field.

PURPOSE OF THESAURUS

The purpose is to provide a controlled structured vocabulary of terms that can be used for indexing information relating to their application. The major purpose of thesaurus are to provide a mean by which the use of terms in a given subject field may be standardized; and to index specialized collections of documents, abstracts, bulletins, current awareness tools, SDI systems and a variety of other bibliographical tools.

TYPES OF THESAURI

Based on the nature of terminology control, there are mainly two types of thesauri; i.e., Controlled thesauri which allow one term (preferred term) to denote a concept for the purpose of indexing and searching; and free language thesauri, which allow use of all terms to denote a concept to be used for indexing and searching.

The controlled thesauri can be maintained manually but free language thesauri require machine maintenance and retrieval.

CONVERTIBLE THESAURUS

A group of information centers with similar subject interests obviously needs a thesaurus, which can ensure easy exchange of information. In such a situation, any well-developed thesaurus of one of the centres may be taken as macro-thesaurus with other centers creating, within the same frame work, micro-thesaurus oriented to their particular needs. Alternatively, each center can develop its own thesaurus independently and can resort to a 'switching' or 'reconciling' thesaurus for interchange purposes. Such a thesaurus is called convertible thesaurus. It is also known as source thesaurus.

STRUCTURE OF THESAURUS

The internal form of individual entries and the arrangement of various entries in relation to one another constitute the structure of a thesaurus. Cross-references make explicit the way in which entries relate to each other in a network of concepts. The different terms in a entry are displayed in the following format:

Descriptor (with scope note whenever needed)

Synonyms and quasi-synonyms

(Displaying equivalence relationship and denoted by the relationship indicated USE / UF (Use for)

Broader Terms

(Displaying hierarchical - super ordinate relationship and denoted by BT)

Narrower Terms

(Displaying hierarchical-subordinate relationship and denoted by NT)

Related Terms

(Displaying associated relationship and denoted by RT)

Top Term

(Displaying the broader class to which the descriptor belongs and denoted by TT)

RELATIONSHIPS BETWEEN TERMS

The inter-relationships between the terms in a thesaurus are brought out by two basic types of relationships:

1. Hierarchical relationships
2. Non-hierarchical relationships

HIERARCHICAL RELATIONSHIPS

Hierarchical relationships refer to super-ordinate and sub-ordinate relationship for a concept. This relationship may be of three types: Genus-species (Generic) relationship; Hierarchical whole - part relationship; and Instance relationship

(i) Genus-Species Relationship

Links genus and species and represents the basis of scientific taxonomic system e.g.

Rodents	Mice
NT Mice	BT Rodents

(ii) Hierarchical Whole-part Relationship

Means that the name of a part implies the name of its whole in any context, e.g.

Cardio - Vascular System	Circulatory System
BT Circulatory System	NT Cardio-Vascular System

(iii) Instance Relationship

Which links proper name with common noun e.g.

Mountain Regions
NT Alps BT Mountain
Mountain
NT Himalayas

Alps
Regions
Himalayas
BT Mountain Regions

NON-HIERARCHICAL RELATIONSHIPS

When two terms are related other than hierarchical, the relationship may be called non-hierarchical relationship. This may be grouped as: Equivalence (or Preferential) relationship and Associative (or affinitive) relationship.

(i) Equivalence Relationship

Usually it refers to the preferred terms and distinguishes such terms from the non-preferred terms. Synonyms, near-synonyms, and quasi-synonyms come under this category. The symbols used to represent these relationships in a thesaurus are USE and UF. e.g.

Disabilities
USE Handicaps

Handicaps
UF Disabilities

Games
USE Sports

Sports
UF Games

(ii) Associative Relationship

This relationship is employed to cover other relationship between terms that are related but are neither consistently hierarchical **nor** equivalent. They are indicated by the code RT.

Birds
RT Ornithology

Ornithology
RT Birds

Indexing
RT Efficiency

Efficiency
RT Indexing

ROLE OF THESAURUS IN INDEXING AND SEARCHING

Thesaurus plays the following two roles:

(i) Prescriptive Role : It prescribes as to what term should be assigned. The 'USE' reference is a prescriptive indicator.

(ii) Suggestive Role : It suggests terms to be considered instead have, or in addition to, etc. The RT is suggestive indicators.

THESAURUS IN POST-COORDINATE INDEXING SYSTEMS

Thesaurus has come into existence as a tool for vocabulary control in post-coordinated indexing system. It helps the indexer in selecting the appropriate terms for indexing, as the indexer may not be familiar with the subject field. Besides providing alternative search paths, a thesaurus aids in choosing term for summation when information on all the aspects of a subject field is required, search has to be made covering all the related aspects. Here, the searcher may not be able to recall all the information that the system can give without the aid of a thesaurus.

THESAURI AND SUBJECT HEADING LISTS

Both thesauri and subject heading lists are vocabulary control devices, but they are used in different situations, the essential characteristics, which differentiate them, are considered as follows:

(a) Subject heading list fulfills the need of pre-coordinate indexes, whereas a thesaurus is designed to meet the specific needs of post-coordinate indexes.

(b) Thesauri generally contain terms that are more specific than those found in conventional subject-heading lists.

(c) A thesaurus normally avoids inverted terms such as 'psychology, children'.

(d) The relationship display is more extensive in the case of thesaurus than in the case of traditional subject heading lists.

(e) The relationships between terms listed in a thesaurus are not transferred to the indexes in many cases. Dictionary catalogues normally provide 'see' and 'see also' references linking the related subject headings.

THESAURO-FACET

This concept has been developed by Jean Aitchison and others for English Electric Company. It is basically a faceted classification, integrated with a thesaurus. Thesauro-facet consists of two sections - (i) faceted classification scheme, and (ii) alphabetical thesaurus. Here, the thesaurus replaces the alphabetical subject index, which normally follows the schedules in a conventional faceted classification. Terms appear twice -once in the schedule and once in the alphabetical thesaurus, the link between two locations being the notation or class number. It can be used in both pre- and post-coordinate indexing system.

CONSTRUCTION OF THESAURUS

For compilation of a thesaurus, the following steps are usually followed:

1. **Determination of scope :** the subject field on which thesaurus is constructed is to be determined.
2. **Determination of characteristics :** A decision has to be taken regarding the following characteristics of a thesaurus:
   (a) the level of specificity
   (b) the level of pre-co-ordination
   (c) the extent of hierarchical and other relationship
   (d) auxiliary precision devices (e.g. links, roles) to be used
   (e) arrangement and layout of the main and auxiliary parts.
3. **Division of subject field into facets :** The main areas or facets of the subject field may be identified with the help of representative books on the subject

and the specialists in the field.

4. **Identification of sources :** The sources from which terms are to be collected should be identified before starting the term collection work. Such sources may include standard reference tools such as encyclopedias, glossaries" etc) classification schemes and thesauri, primary and secondary periodicals etc.

5. **Collection and selection of terms :** Each of the source may be scanned for collection of relevant terms which will serve as the descriptor should be chosen. A term record should be prepared for each of the term selected in a specially designed term record card. An example of simple term record is shown below :

Term	Microforms
Context	Reprography
Characteristics	By form
Definition/Scope note	A miniature replication of document
Synonyms	Microcopies
Broader Term	Data, media
Narrower Term	Micro-transparencies Macro-opaques
Related Terms	Micropho
Source	McGrawhill Dictionary of Scientific and Technical Terms, New York, McGrawhill 1974.

6. **Determination of Relation :** determination of interrelation between the terms is the most significant step, either inductive or deductive. After determining all the relationship between these should be noted down in appropriate place of the term record.

7. **Preparation of entries :** An entry should not be prepared for each descriptor using necessary abbreviations or symbols.

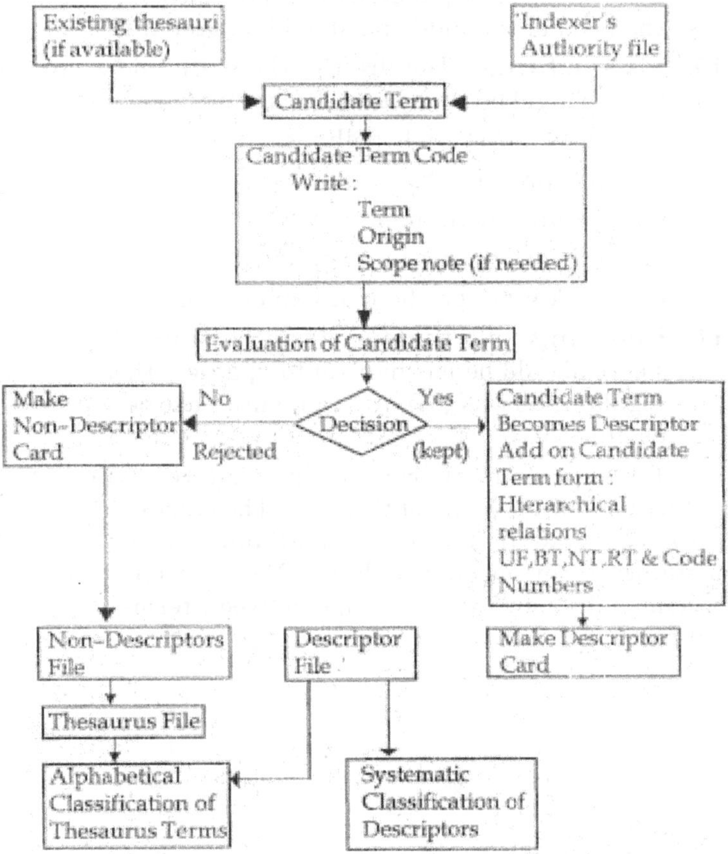

Thesaurus Construction Flow Chart

8. **Arrangement of main entry :** When the main part is alphabetical, the entries for descriptor and non-preferred terms are all arranged in alphabetical order. In case of classified main part, the terms are arranged in a hierarchy as in a classification scheme. Scope notes, synonyms and related terms are added wherever necessary.

9. **Preparation of Auxiliary Part :** The auxiliary part

necessary to supplement the main part and to meet the need of the indexing should be prepared.

10. **Final editing :** The draft of the main and auxiliary parts should be tested and checked on following points:
    (a) Word forms and spellings
    (b) Reciprocal entries
    (c) Arrangement of entries
    (d) Indentions, spacing and layout
    (e) Link between the main and auxiliary part.
11. **Updating :** No thesaurus can be static document. There should be mechanism to update a thesaurus at regular intervals so that it can continue to be a dynamic useful tool.

Thesaurus is increasingly used to handle the production and updating of thesauri. Thesaurus completely up-to-date and- if it is to be available tool it must be constantly amended and updated. New concepts must be accommodated, and relationships between terms are to be modified.

17

Thesaurofacet

The 'English Electric Company's Classification for Engineering' was the largest faceted scheme designed by the members of CRG (Classification Research Group). The first edition of this scheme appeared in 1958 and third in 1961. With the advent of computer technology the company started investigating the possibilities of using computer techniques post-coordinate indexing. In 1969 the scheme was accordingly compiled by Jean Aitchinson and published under the title 'The *Thesaurofacet*: a thesaurus and faceted classification for engineering and related subjects'.

THE FORMAT OF THESAUROFACET

The thesaurofacet comprises of two parts - (i) a thesaurus and (ii) classification schedules.

(i) The Thesaurus

The thesaurus functions as an alphabetical subject index to approach the classification schedules. The specific term approach is used for this purpose. For e.g., if a user has a specific term in mind, e.g. television camera tubes, he may consult the thesaurus at this term, wherein he would be directed to see the class number MCE in the schedules. Thesaurus also indicates Related Terms (RT), Used For items (UF) including synonyms, near synonyms and alternative word forms, such as Broader Terms (BT).

Example:

Television camera tubes MCE class number	
UF	Camera Tubes (television)
	Emitrons
	Iconoscopes
	Image Orthicons
	Pick up tubes (television)
RT	Photomultipliers
	Phototubes
	Television Camera
BT (A)	Television Apparatus

Additional Broader (BT) and Narrower Terms (NT)

The thesaurus also gives information about such concepts, which are broader or narrower in hierarchy than the index terms. An (A) in brackets is given after the BT or NT to show that the relationship occurs in an auxiliary or additional hierarchy.

Example

Jets	CWJ
RT	Jet Condensers
	Jet dispersal Values
	Jet Pumps
NT (A)	Jets (hover craft)
	Plasma jets

Additional Related Terms (RT)

Related Terms (RT) are given in the thesaurus for concepts which are related to the index terms other than hierarchy. Related terms frequently occurs in widely seperated subject fields, because the relationship between them is not easily displayed in the basic classification schedules.

Example:

Biolers

RT Steam Pipes

Lasers

RT Coherence

(ii) Classification Schedules

In this part, the whole field of science and technology is first grouped into conventional mean subjects. For e.g.

A	General Concept
B	Science
BA	Mathematical Sciences
C	Physics
I	Technology

Then, within each broad subject facet, principles are applied. In a given subject - field, facet analysis is used to group. The terms into fundamental facets or categories such as - Entities - things parts; and Attributes - properties, processes; to application and effects. The concepts within fundamental categories may be grouped into sub-facets. Terms within sub-facets and fundamental facets are arranged in hierarchical and arrays. Cross-references are also given to make visual display of related concepts, which are enumerated elsewhere in the schedule. All such concepts are preceded by an asterisk '*'

DJ Electricity

(UF Electric properties)

* Atmospheric electricity IJV

* Electrical Engineering J3.

A thesaurus mentions a number of related terms in one place but is not able to show the exact nature of their relationship with the index term. They are the terms of unspecified relationship. The hierarchical display in the schedules of a classification provides a view of the exact number of relationship. The thesaurofacet combines the above two relational display techniques.

For e.g., if one is looking for information on 'electrification of railways' and looks up under the term 'electrification' he is likely to come across the following entry in the thesaurus part;

Electrification (Railways)

Use Electric Railways

Taking the above clue one gets the following display under the referred index term;

Electric Railways R71

UF	Electrification (Railways)
RT	Conductor Rails
	Current Collection Equipment (Traction)
	Electric Locomotives
	Electric Vehicles
	Supply Lines (Traction)
BT (A)	Electrically Operated Devices

R71 mentioned against the index term serves as a direct link between the above display in the thesaurus part and the hierarchical display of the same concept in the classified part. Using the above link, one would get the following display in the classified part:

R Transport Engineering

....

....

....

R5 Railway Engineering

By Control System

R7 Railway Control Systems

By special railway systems

R71 Electric Railways

	* Conductor Rails	R5L
	* Current Collecting Equipment (Traction)	R67
	* Electric Locomotives	R6H
	* Supply Lines (Traction)	R5J
R7K	Tramcars	
R7L	Trolley Buses	
R7N	Underground Railways	
R7P	Elevated Railways	
R78	Monorail	
R7S	Fast Transit Rail System	
R7T	Rack and Pinion Railways	

The above two displays together bring into focus different types of relationships. In the thesaurus display, only one BT(A), 'electrically operated devices' has been mentioned while in the classification schedule, display of a number of broader terms of the selected index i.e. 'electric railways' are automatically seen. In the classificatory hierarchy, 'railway control systems', 'railway engineering' and 'transport engineering' are all broader terms. In the same way, narrower terms are also displayed. In the thesaurus display, however the BT(A) was mentioned because it occurs in an additional hierarchy which the schedule display is not able to show. Here the relationship of RTs with the index term remains unspecified. But a reference to the relevant portion of the schedule, through the link of the class number, brings out the nature of relationship of two wants to find out the exact relationship of two RTs mentioned in the thesaurus display, viz., 'electric vehicles' and 'electric locomotives' then he gets the following display in the schedule:

R2	Vehicle Engineering
R2C	Vehicles
	....

....

....

R2M	Electric Vehicles	
	* Electric Automobiles	R4H
	* Electric Locomotives	R6H
	* Electric Rocket Engines	RU
	* Electric Trucks	R3N
	* Marine Electric Propulsion	RAT
R2P	Amphibious Vehicles	

In this way one can move along different hierarchical and spot out new and exact relationships.

SYNTHESIS

The thesaurofacet enumerates in its schedule not only isolate terms and isolate numbers but also synthesized or compound subjects and synthesized class numbers. Such terms in the schedule are indicated by the use of 'synth' and in the thesaurus part the constituent concepts of such synthesized terms are indicated by the prefix V.

Example - Synthesis: Classification schedules:

LL Oscillators

By frequency

Combine with notation from frequency schedules

e.g.	LL/CF2	Audio frequency Oscillators
	LL/DY2	Radio frequency Oscillators
	LL/DY5	Very low frequency Oscillators
	LL/DYC	Very high frequency Oscillators
	LL/DYF	Microwave Oscillators

Synthesis: Thesaurus entry

Microwave Oscillators LL/DYF

Synthesis:

SRT	Microwaves	
SBT	Oscillators	Constituent terms
BT (A)	Microwave	
	Devices	
	Radar apparatus	Additional Broader Terms

NOTATION

Notation is mixed consisting of Roman Capital letters and Indo-Arabic Numerals (omitting 0 and 1) is also used to indicate synthesis. The notation is ordinal and not hierarchical, which means that the notation is not structural and does not reflect sub-divisions and hierarchies. This type of notation facilitates interpolation at any point in the schedule and enables greater hospitality.

DRAWBACKS IN THE FORMAT OF THESAUROFACET

1. Only a very few cross-references are given in the schedules. There is no differentiation in the schedules between BT, NT and RT cross-references.
2. The main part is arranged alphabetically and notations are omitted in the cross-references in the main part.
3. There is no alphabetical index. Therefore, spelling variants, especially inverted forms have to be included in the main part. This has located the main part with information that does not fit in these.

FURTHER READINGS

1. Ghosh, S.B. and Satpathi, J.N) *Subject indexing systems: concepts, methods and techniques. Calcutta: IASLIC, 1998.*
2. Guha, B., *Documentation and information. Calcutta: World, 1982.*
3. *Khanna, J.K., Communicating Knowledge. Delhi: Research, 1996.*
4. Riaz, Muhammad. *Modern techniques of documentation and information work. Delhi: Royal, 1972.*

18

Vocabulary Control

Indexing is one of the techniques used for storing and retrieving information, so that it is easily accessible to readers with least effort and time. An indexing language is essentially a controlled language. Any such language will have certain degree of artificiality in it in the sense that it is different from a natural language, which is designed and created for a specific purpose to bring the users interest and the information retrieval system closer. The vocabulary of a retrieval system exerts a considerable influence on its performance and on the search strategy. To exercise control, a select list of index terms is prepared for indexing purpose. The outcome of terminology control comes in the form of standard word list, also called Thesaurus.

MEANING OF VOCABULARY CONTROL

Information retrieval implies location of documents and/or information with reference to the information needs of the users. To do this effectively it is necessary for the documents to be analysed conceptually and to represent the concepts by a set of term. Terms used to represent concept are referred to as Keywords, Kernel terms, Index terms or,descriptors. A set of descriptors used by an information retrieval system is called as the vocabulary of the system. Generally, the vocabulary used in a system is a "Controlled

Vocabulary". The use of a controlled vocabulary in a contrast to the use of a natural language is essential to ensure efficient retrieval performance of the system.

Thus a controlled vocabulary may be described or defined as "a list of words or term showing their relationships and indicating way in which they may usefully be combined to give the class intersections or in set to be interested in". In other words a certain degree of structure is introduced in a controlled vocabulary so that term whose meanings are related are brought together or linked in some way.

OBJECTIVES OF VOCABULARY CONTROL

The objectives of vocabulary control with in an information retrieval system are as follows :

1. To promote consistent representation of the subject matter by indexers and searchers, thereby avoiding the dispersion of related materials, through control (merging) of synonymous and nearly synonymous expressions by distinguishing among homonyms/ homographs.
2. To facilitate the conduct of a comprehensive search on some topic by linking together terms whose meanings are related paradigmatically or syntagmatically.

NEED OF VOCABULARY CONTROL

Vocabulary control is necessary for information retrieval system. If the indexers represent the concepts discussed in a document using the term of a natural language, retrieval will not be very successful. This is because of the fact that a natural language contains a large amount of synonyms, quasi-synonyms, homonyms, eponyms, acronyms, ambiguous terms etc. Hence, if vocabulary control is not exercised, different indexers or one and the same indexer at different times is likely to use a different set of term for representing the thought content of similar documents (i.e. documents dealing with the same subject) on the one hand and to use a different set of term for representing the same subject at the time of searching. This in turn would result in a "Mis Match" and thus affect information retrieval. In other words, a certain degree of vocabulary control is desirable, if not essential. Examples of synonyms, homonyms, eponyms, "acronyms etc., are given below.

Synonyms

CELIN = Vitamin C , .

Athletes foot = Tinea Pedis

Christmas Disease = Haemophilia B

Pulmonary Tuberculosis = Pthisis

Quasi Synonyms

Genetics = Heredity

Accuracy = Precision

Eponyms

Addison - Biermer Disease: Pernicious anemia

Homonyms

Mercury may represent planet, Mercury or Mercury metal

Acronyms, Abbreviation

ACTH FOR Andre no - corticatrophpic hormone

USSR FOR Union of the Soviet Socialistic Republic

Functions of Vocabulary Control

The main functions of vocabulary control are as follow:

1. One obvious result of lack of vocabulary control is inconsistency in the representation of identical subject matter. By this we mean that a particular topic may be represented in many different ways in different documents or by different indexers. To take a very simple example, the same 'pathological condition may be represented by one index as 'pulmonary tuberculosis' and by another as 'tuberculosis of the lung'. In an uncontrolled vocabulary situation the

searcher must think of all synonymous words or expressions in order to find all relevant literature on a particular topic. This place an additional -burden on the searcher and it is by no means certain that he will be able to come up with all synonyms. Example- the concept of level (of a chemical substance) in blood might be variously represented in text as:

blood levels, blood concentration
serum levels, serum concentration

2. One of the major functions of the controlled vocabulary is to control synonyms, that is, to specify which of several synonymous expressions is to be used by indexers and searchers and thus to avoid the separation of identical subject matter under different terms in the system. Such control is achieved simply by choosing one of the possible alternatives, the "preferred term" and referring to it -see or use - from the variants under which certain users may be likely to approach the system. It should be obvious that the synonym selected as the preferred term, that under which documents are actually indexed and searched for, must be the one under which the majority of system users are likely to look first. Although "synonym control" is the expression most commonly used.

3. The controlled vocabulary also distinguishes among homographs that is, words with identical spelling but different meaning, usually by means of a parenthetical qualifier or scope note. Thus, MERCURY (mythological) tells us that this term is to be used exclusively for a mythological character and not for a planet, a metal, a car or any other possible context. By controlling synonyms, near synonyms and quasi synonyms and distinguishing among homographs the controlled vocabulary avoids the dispersion of like subject matter and the collocation of unlike subject matter. In this way, it helps to achieve the objective of

consistent representation of subject matter in indexing and searching.

4. Another major function of vocabulary control is to link together terms that are semantically related in order to facilitate the conduct of comprehensive searches. It would for example, be extremely difficult to conduct a search on Cereal production in the Middle East if one had to think of all terms that might indicate cereals and all those which might indicate Middle East.

DESCRIPTORS AND CONTROLLED VOCABULARY

Effective searching and retrieval can be gained through the use of natural language and controlled vocabulary. The idea of controlled vocabulary is centred round the use of descriptors in representation of a volume of information that may help in indexing the conceptual access to required sources of information.

A descriptor is a term or a set of terms used to surrogate the concept, i.e., an entity, a property, an action, a space and time and any other kindered objects.

METHODS FOR GENERATION OF DESCRIPTORS

A descriptor may be generated by the following approaches:

1. Terms usually taken from title of abstract of technical document.
2. Terms extracted from the text of a document or an abstract, by man or machine in some more careful ways, but without any vocabulary control.
3. Terms extracted from the text but with some vocabulary control.
4. Terms which may not directly form part of a text, but which are equivalent to what is given in vocabulary control device.

DEVICES USED FOR VOCABULARY CONTROL

The major devices for vocabulary Control are Thesaurus; Standard List of Subject Headings; Scheme of Classification with artificial notation.

(i) Thesaurus

A thesaurus is defined as - "a compilation of words and phrases showing synonyms, hierarchical and other relationships and dependencies, the function of which is to provide a standardized vocabulary for information storage and retrieval systems".

The functions of thesaurus are to define and list valid and invalid elements of the vocabulary and to exhibit the relationship among the valid terms. Many of the problems observed earlier with natural language - homographs, synonyms, generic searches, and even false coordinations - are dealt within the structure of the thesaurus.

In a controlled thesaurus, vocabulary control is affected by following norms:

1. Only one term out of all possible synonyms and quasi-synonyms is selected as the descriptor.
2. The scope of the term is deliberately restricted to a selected meaning which is best suited for an indexing system. The scope is clearly indicated in a scope note whenever required.
3. Spellings, numbers (singular/ plural) and word forms are standardized.
4. A definite rule is followed for compound terms.
5. Homographs (homonyms) are avoided as far as possible and differentiated by qualifiers, if at all used.

Most index terms in a thesaurus are uniterms or single concept terms. Another key point of a thesaurus is that it indicates the relationships among terms. This is achieved by showing under each term the broader, more narrow and related terms. The symbols to express relationships in thesauri are:

SN	Scope note
USE	Equivalent to "see" reference
UF	Use for, the reciprocal of USE
BT	Broader term in a hierarchical way
NT	Narrow term, in a hierarchical way, the reciprocal of BT
RT	Related term, expressing any useful relationship other than BT / NT

The structure of a typical thesaurus is presented in a chart form :

Barley	Factories	
BT Grain	UF Plants (industry)	
Cereals	Grains	
USE Grain	UF Cereals	
	BT Crops	
Corn	NT Barley	RT Flour
BT Grain	Corn	Flour Mills
	Maize	Harvesting
	Oats	Milling
	Rye	Threshing
	Wheat	

Plants (Botany)

Plants (Industry)

USE Factories

(ii) Subject Headings

The indexer in his own way cannot practice subject indexing as the entries in a subject index are made in accordance with specific rules governing their choice, style and terminology. The lists of subject headings aim to provide one form of subject headings under which all documents on a given subject can be listed. Thus, this function shows that it is also a kind of vocabulary control. There are very popular important and well-known lists of subject headings they are as follows

a. Library of Congress List of Subject Headings
b. Sears List of Subject Headings

(a) Library of Congress List of Subject Headings

The first edition of Library of Congress (LC) list appeared in 1911. In this only those subject headings were included which were chosen for the dictionary catalogue. Symbol 'sa' indicate 'see also'; V means make 'see' reference from; and 'xx' indicates that 'see also' reference be made from the heading preceeded by it.

From 11th edition in 1988, 'see' and 'see also' references and the complementary 'xx' and V were replaced by the thesaurus conventions BT, NT, RT, UF, USE and SA.

This indicates that some kind of control is made on the vocabulary. Example :

Chemistry [may subdivided geographically]

[QD]

SA	headings beginning with the word chemical
BT	Physical sciences
NT	Acids
	Agricultural Chemistry
	Etc.......

(b) Sears List of Subject Headings

The Sears List for Subject Headings with almost eight decades of progressive history behind it is now a very familiar tool of subject cataloguing in small and medium size, libraries in most of the English speaking countries. Its regular editions have kept the Sears List rejuvenated. On this account, it keeps thriving in times of too quickly shifting sands of subject cataloguing.

Seventeenth edition (2000) is the third consecutive edition under the editorship of Dr. Joseph Miller who joined as edition in 1992 succeeding Martha Mooney. It may be noted that since the Sears 15, the first edition by Dr. Miller, the Sears List has seen spectacular changes. These are namely, diversion of the headings, thesaurus format display and now the merger of the list of commonly used subdivisions. In this edition, policy changes and technical improvements initiated in the previous two editions have come a full circle.

Example :

Libraries, College and University

x College libraries; Libraries, University; University Libraries

xx Colleges and Universities

College Libraries

See

Libraries, College and University

Libraries, University

See

Libraries, college and university

Colleges and Universities

See also Libraries, College and University

Sears now uses thesaurus type cross-references BT, NT, RT, SA, USE and UF. There is a detailed explanation of how these relate to the previously used 'see' and 'see also' references, which are still recommended for 'cross-references' in general. References from RT to RT are made both ways only if both headings are in use in the catalogue, and upward references from NT to BT are not made.

Example :

Bicycles and bicycling

USE Bicycles

Cycling

Bicycles

UF Bicycles and bicycling

NT Mountain bikes

RT Cycling

Advantages of the List

(1) Standard lists of subject headings guide a catalogue as to which of the term among the synonymous terms is to be preferred in a catalogue entry.

(2) The list also indicates the rendering of the subject heading, i.e., the sequence of the terms in a multi-worded heading.

(3) The list also indicate the reference to be made (see and see also) from term (s) not used to the one used.

Limitations

(1) The lists are always found inadequate.

(2) Most of the lists are based on the practices in one or a few libraries. Their decisions are either based on some convenience or arbitrary. Hence, create problems many a time.

(3) The lists need constant revision, failing which its purpose is defeated.

(4) As the intention of the subject increases, the subject heading becomes complex. Most of the lists try to avoid complex subject headings.

(5) Subject heading lists proved to be 'insufficient' for bibliographies and documentation lists.

(6) Creation of new terms, new terms for old subjects, homonyms and synonyms pose a lot of problems in keeping the lists up-to-date.

(iii) Classification Schemes

The functions of classification schemes are more or less similar to that of thesauri. Classification schemes organize concepts in a logical systematic manner and indicate the interrelationships between concepts. They reflect the equivalence hierarchical and non-hierarchical relationship that is incident among the concepts. However, function of a classification system is generally confined to a library atmosphere. It acts as a tool for the intellectual organization of documents on the shelves of an almirah and surrogates in a catalogue. While both classification scheme and thesauri are vocabulary control devices, there is a difference in arrangement and display of terms. In the classification scheme, the terms are presented in a hierarchical fashion with or without notation. In other words, notation is not an essential characteristic for a classification scheme, for example: the following two arrangements of terms can be considered as part of a classification scheme.

Arrangement 1		Arrangement 2
Vertebrates	V	Vertibralis
Pisces	V_1	Pisces
Lung-fishes	V_{11}	Lung-fishes
Amphibia	V_2	Amphibia
Reptiles	V_3	Reptiles
Snakes	V_{31}	Snakes
Aves/ Birds	V_4	Aves/ Birds
Mammals	V_5	Mammals
Man	V_{51}	Man

The classified part is supplemented by an alphabetical Index to show a user where in the classification scheme a particular term appears. In case, the scheme is without a notation, the index would refer to the page on which the term occurs - with illustrates.

INFLUENCE OF VOCABULARY ON THE PERFORMANCE OF A RETRIEVAL SYSTEM

The important requirements of a controlled vocabulary are perhaps best illustrated by considering the types of failures that might occur in a search due, directly or indirectly, to defects or limitations in the vocabulary. These failures are of three major types:

1. Those due to lack of specificity in the vocabulary
2. Those due to ambiguous or spurious relationships among terms
3. Those due to lack of adequate structure.

In a controlled vocabulary system, lack of specificity is likely to be the most important source of failure. The specificity of the vocabulary is the single most important factor influencing the precision with which a search can be conducted. It is true, in fact that the major factor controlling the level of precision that can be achieved in a retrieval system is the degree of specificity in the vocabulary.

Ambiguous and spurious relationships among terms are another source of precision failures. Although, some failures of this kind are likely to occur in any post-coordinate system.

The third possible source of failure is inadequate structure in the vocabulary. The controlled vocabulary must help the searcher by bringing to his attention all the terms that would be needed to conduct a comprehensive search in some subject area. Unless it does the specific term search, the vocabulary does not give the searcher maximum assistance, and there is a danger that he may overlook some of the terms that would be needed to conduct a comprehensive search on the subject.

The essential unity of the functions of a thesaurus, subject heading list and classification scheme may be indicated in the following manner.

Uncontrolled Vocabularies	Alphabetical Subject Heading Authority lists	Three level Word Thesauri threes	Multi level Hierarchical Classification

As one moves from left to right in the figure, one finds that the vocabulary control devices have an increasing degree of organization and increasing delineation of relationship and this suggests that the response of an information retrieval system can progressively be improved by using devices which are well structured.

REFERENCES

1. Ghosh, S.B. and Satpathi, J.N. *Subject indexing systems: concepts, methods and techniques. Calcutta: IASLIC, 1998.*
2. Lancaster, F.W., *Information Retrieval Systems: characteristics, testing and evaluation. New York: John Wiley, 1979.*
3. Riaz, Muhammad, *Modern techniques of documentation and information work. Delhi Royal, 1972.*

19

Evaluation of An Indexing System

Any information system exists to provide the seeker of information the document, which bears his information or answers his query. An index is an operational tool that helps the information system to achieve this objective. Indexing involves the content analysis of the documents and the translation of this analysis into a particular vocabulary. A library catalogue is a typical example of an index. It helps the user in accessing the documents, which may contain his information. An index at the back of a book helps a reader to trace a particular name or concept or subject discussed or mentioned in the book. Similarly, a bibliographic index

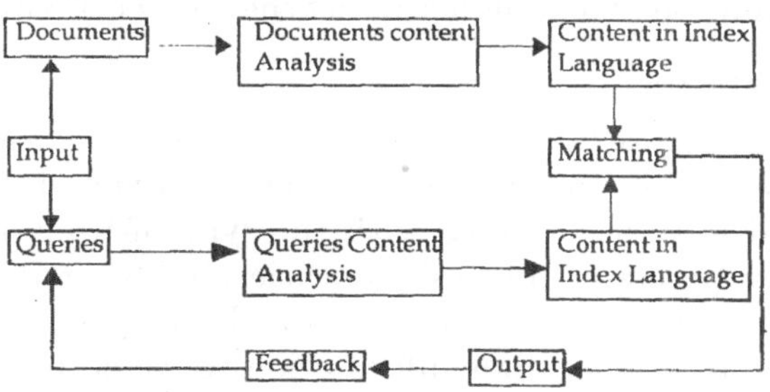

Information Retrieval System

provides information about the documents on a particular subject.

FACTORS AFFECTING INDEXES

There are a number of factors, which have direct or indirect effect on the indexes. They are as follows:

1. Indexer

Indexers who actually analyze the documents and assign them index numbers or verbal presentation prepares the indexes. In case, he is providing an index number using a classification scheme, then he should be intelligent enough to understand the subject well and thus denote the subject fully in the notational form. If the indexer is not able to identify the subject content intellectually, then the indexes thus prepared will not be able to retrieve the right document at the right time, which will create noise in the system.

2. Pre-coordination and Post-coordination of Terms

The terms determined for representing a subject through indexes are either pre-coordinated or post-coordinated at different stages. In case of pre-coordinate indexing, the sequencing of terms is predetermined, which limits the researchers approach point. Whereas the indexes prepared under post-coordinate indexing, also pose problems due to the free terms, which again need some type of pre-coordination. Thus, the index prepared using any one of the above mentioned techniques affect the users utilizing it also.

3. Type of User

The indexes prepared are always purpose oriented. It exists to satisfy the user requirements. Every index thus prepared is in accordance with the type of user, it has to deal with. In case of university libraries, indexing using chain procedure is sufficient but when dealing with special libraries, where speedier information retrieval is essential, much precise and computer based indexing techniques are to be needed.

4. Indexing Language Used

While preparing an index standardization of the selected keywords is necessary which is attained by the use of an indexing language. Indexing language is of two types. Derived Term type and Assigned Term type". The derived term type takes the terms for the document and assigned term type is the one in which the indexer constructs the index terms. Any flow on the part of the indexer while structuring logic or sense in indexing language will produce irrelevant output.

5. Number of Documents Indexed

Indexes have an adverse effect on the number of documents indexed. If a small number of documents are to be indexed, it can be carefully analyzed and properly indexed but when the documents are large in quantity, it is difficult to hold concentration, which could lead to inaccurate indexes.

6. Type of Documents indexed

Another important factor affecting indexes is the type of documents indexed. Indexing of simple subject contents is easier, whereas complex subject material is difficult to index, as it would require proper understanding of the contents. Any error in choice of correct term would lead to unwanted retrieval.

7. Computerized Indexes

Computer is efficient enough to prepare indexes as instructed, without wastage of time and labour. But in case of complex subjects the computer can analyze the specific subject content to produce effective indexes, which again leads to broad indexes that reduce the efficiency of indexes prepared through computers.

NEED FOR EVALUATION OF INDEXING SYSTEM

The main purpose for which an indexing system is evaluated is :

- To reveal the strength and also the weaknesses of an indexing system.
- To achieve maximum efficiency of the indexes prepared.
- To increase the usefulness of the indexing system
- To find out the social benefits that occurs from the indexing system.
- To find out the economical aspects of the systems such as cost involved etc.
- To find out measures to be taken for improving or changing the system.

CRITERIA FOR EVALUATION

An indexing system may be evaluated on the basis of the following criteria:

Cost; Quality; Cost of Effectiveness; Response Time; Precision; Recall; Exhaustivity; Specificity; and Novelty Ratio.

(i) Cost

An efficient indexing system provides maximum benefit to the users at the least cost. Cost not only in terms of money, but the amount of labour involved in retrieving the documents containing information is also taken into account. Thus, if the adopted system is of reasonable cost and the efforts required are also bearable only then can it be termed as efficient, otherwise not.

(ii) Quality

The quality of an indexing system is an important criterion that affects its efficiency. If the documents indexed are retrieved easily, it is said to be of good quality. The quality of the system depends on factors as coverage, recall, precision, and accuracy of the data. An indexing system should consist of all these aspects only then can its quality be regarded as being user oriented.

(iii) Cost Effectiveness

The cost effectiveness should include the cost of every relevant item and the cost per new relevant item. Retaining the optimum quality, lesser the cost per relevant item or per new relevant item, the more efficient an indexing system will be considered.

(iv) Response Time

The time taken by an indexing system to respond to answers query, would also determine the efficiency of that system. Quick retrieval of relevant documents is expected of an efficient indexing system. But it should also be remembered that the response time depends on the type of query. Some queries take less time; while others take a long time to retrieve such documents as may provide answer to query.

(v) Precision

When a search is carried out in response to a query, sometimes the user is able to retrieve the correct document and in some cases he lands up with a wrong retrieval. The quality of searching the right document accurately is said to be the precision value of the system. For any indexing system, the amount of relevant material retrieved, gives us the precision ratio, as being the percentage of the total amount retrieved, in one search, which is calculated as:

$$\text{Precision} = \frac{\text{No. of relevant items retrieved}}{\text{Total no. of items retrieved}} \times 100$$

The situation can be depicted as follows:

Documents	*Retrieved*	*Not-retrieved*	*Total*
Relevant	a	b	a + b
Not relevant	c	d	c + d
Total	a + c	b + d	a + b + c + d

$$\text{Now precision ration} = \frac{a}{a + c} \times 100$$

If a single search retrieves ten documents out of which six are relevant and the rest are irrelevant, the precision ratio may be calculated as

$$\text{Precision ration} = \frac{6}{10} \times 100 = 60\%\ 10$$

(vi) Recall

Recall is the retrieval of relevant documents by the system. Recall ratio means as to how many relevant documents among the total relevant documents have been retrieved by the indexing system. Recall ratio is calculated as:

$$\text{Recall Ration} = \frac{\text{No. of relevant items retrieved}}{\text{Total no. of relevant items}} \times 100$$

Or

$$\text{Recall Ration} = \frac{a}{a + b} \times 100$$

Suppose there are 100 relevant documents in all in a file and the index is able to retrieve only 75 of them, and misses 25, then the recall ratio is:

$$\text{Recall Ration} = \frac{75}{75 + 25} \times 100 = 75\%$$

It is difficult to calculate the recall value of the system, as it is not possible to know the total number of relevant documents in a collection.

The better the recall value of a system, the efficient it will be, as it will retrieve maximum number of relevant documents from the entire collection. The recall ratio and precision ration act as a filter in keeping away the unwanted material from being retrieved, thus increase the retrieval efficiency of the system.

(vii) Exhaustivity

The extent to which an indexing system satisfies the various approaches of a user, will show its exhaustivity i.e., the more exhaustive the indexing will be, larger will be the number of entries in it. Let us take the case of a document dealing with "technical assistance to South Africa". If we prepare an entry only by the technical assistance, which is the main theme of the document, the index will not have comprehensive coverage but if it prepares entries on ILO, technical assistance and South Africa its coverage would be exhaustive as it. Will now be in a position to cover all the approaches of the users. High level of exhaustivity increases the recall value reducing the precision value and a low level of exhaustivity decreases the recall value and increases the precision value, affecting the retrieval efficiency of the system.

(viii) Specificity

The specificity of the system depends on the indexing language brought into use. If the index terms are co-extensive with the concept of the document and is able to describe it fully, then the indexing is specific. The more comprehensive an indexing language will be, the more specific the terms would be, likewise the smaller the size of the vocabulary used, the lower will be the specificity of the indexes.

(ix) Novelty Ratio

It is the proportion of nascent or new documents, which were brought to the attention of the seekers of information for the first time. Out of the total number of relevant documents :

$$\text{Novelty Ration} = \frac{\text{Relevant references not yet known to the users}}{\text{Relevant references retrieved}}$$

An efficient indexing system will bring to the attention of the users more of such document and thus give novel or new or nascent information.

Other Measures

Three other measures, which were proposed, are as

(i) Coverage Ratio

Coverage Ration =

(ii) Relative Recall

$$\text{Relative Recall} = \frac{\text{Total relevant items examined by user after search}}{\text{Total relevant items user would have liked to examine}}$$

(iii) Cost Per Relevant Items Retrieved Ratio

Another measure for the efficiency of a system may be stated with following formula :

$$C_R =$$

Where C_R = Cost per relevant item

C = Cost of Search

r = No. of Relevant items retrieved

x = No. of irrelevant items retrieved

f = Total cost of retrieving on irrelevant citation

C R F x Relevant items retrived

Total relevant items known

to user before search

The different measures discussed so far for determining the efficiency of an indexing system have evolved from time to time according to the type of document in use and the requirement of the users. In order to provide better service, a regular evaluation of the existing indexing system should be adopted, yielding high level of efficiency.

REFERENCES

1. Guha, B., *Documentation and Information - 2nd rev. ed. - Calcutta: World Press 1983.*
2. Khan, M.T.M., *Information Organization and Communication. New Delhi: Ess Ess, 1998.*
3. Lancaster, F.W., *Information Retrieval Systems: Characteristics, Testing and Evaluation, New York: John Willey, 1979.*
4. Prasher, R.G., *Index and Indexing Systems. Delhi: Medallion, 1989.*

Part IV
Abstracting

20

Abstracting

The proliferation in the universe of knowledge, the ever-growing volume of periodical literature, the growing inter disciplinary character of most fields of search, the explosive growth of technical report publications and the wide communication of pre-prints, drafts and limited distribution of papers, strongly emphasize the need of current awareness of the literature in even a very limited subject field. Catalogues, bibliographies and indexes ensure some degree of bibliographical control and help users to find what is relevant to needs. However, these tools provide only the bare details of author, title and location, hence information about the subject content of the document cannot be fully ascertained. What required is the essence or summary of the subject of the document to ensure proper selection. This essence or summary of the document is loosely termed its abstract. Abstract acts as a valuable retrieval media and current awareness tool.

An abstract is a brief statement of the essential content of the original or an indication of the characteristics of the original or accompanied by bibliographical details, its purpose being to draw attention to the information contained in the original and provide a sufficient basis to the reader to judge whether or not he wants to consult the original. Allen

Kent has put it: "An abstract is a summary of a publication or article accompanied by an adequate bibliographical description to enable the publication or article to be traced". According to Herman M. Weisman -"An abstract is an announcement medium whose objective is to provide knowledge of and an ordered and logical access to new primary literature. It can serve as a tool for both input to and retrieval from a system's information store". "An abstract is an abbreviated, accurate representation of document."

NEED FOR ABSTRACTING

The factors that are responsible for growing need of abstracting may be identified as: Information explosion/Rate of literature growth; Language factor - It helps overcoming language barrier; Time saving-saves time; facilitates literature search; Relevancy of documents can be judged; Abstracts promote current awareness; Interdisciplinary nature of subjects; and Diversity of documents.

PURPOSE OF ABSTRACTING

In addition to the above, abstracts serve the purpose of providing abstracting services; facilitating selection of documents; aiding in preparation of indexes; aiding in purpose of reviews and bibliographies; avoiding duplication in research work. Information abstract can serve as original tracing the development of a subject and helpful in retrospective search.

PARTS OF AN ABSTRACT

A typical Abstract consist off main parts i.e.,. A citation; and The Abstract proper.

The Citation is of the document, which is abstracted. The document may be an article in a periodical, a book or monograph, a patent, a standard, a paper in a conference proceeding etc. The abstractor should describe the document in the citation in such a way that it becomes possible for the reader it identify and locate the document easily.

The second part i.e. the Abstract proper, complete standardization is not possible in this part. But certain rules and guiding principles, when followed by the abstractor, could make his product more acceptable to readers. Some of them are as follows:

GUIDING PRINCIPLES FOR ABSTRACTING

Certain guiding principles are identified for proper abstracting. These are :

(i) Purpose : A statement on the goals, objectives and the aims of the research or we can say why and what of the study. This statement should be included in both the informative and indicative abstracts.

(ii) Scope : The extent and coverage of the work is reported in qualitative and/or quantitative terms like 'brief and 'exhaustive' may be used to characterize the original. The time period covered and/or the number of documents reviewed etc/Sin the scope.

(iii) Method : The techniques or means employed to achieve the previously stated purpose. It includes materials, components and apparatus etc.

(iv) Results : Highlights the most significant findings or the outcome of applying the methods named. The significant quantitative data should be provided.

(v) Conclusions : States the most conclusions or interpretation of the results. Care should be taken that this abbreviated statement does not imply concepts or conclusions broader than those supported in the original.

The basic criteria of abstract are clarity of content and preciseness, and the lucidity of expression.

EXAMPLE OF A TYPICAL ABSTRACT

Now let us look at a typical abstract and try to see how far the points discussed above are reflected in it. The following is an abstract taken from the 'Chemical Abstracts'.

Citation

Influence of Zinc deficiency on dry material digestibility in ruminants. W.J. Miller, G.W. Powell and J.M. Heirs, Jr.(University of Georgia, Athens). Journal of Dairy Science 49(8), 1012-13 (1966) (English)

Purpose

Since it was known that when fed at the same level of intake as normal Calves, Zn-deficient calves grew at a much slower rate and required more feed per unit of weight gain. A study was conducted to determine.

Methodology

If Zn-deficiency affected the digestibility of dry matter in the diet of goats and calves, Dry matter digestibility of a purified diet was determined with 2 Zn-deficient and 2 control goats in 47 day total collection periods. A comparable experiment was conducted with calves using 39 day collection periods.

Result

Zn-deficiency, did not affect the digestibility of dry matter.

CONCLUSION

Thus the reduced feed efficiency in Zri-deficiericy animals is caused by a reduced utilization of digested nutrients.

In this abstract, first portion is a complete citation of an article published in a periodical. In the abstract proper, the four components of the abstract namely purpose, methodology, results and conclusions are clearly discernible and they also occur in that sequence.

TYPES OF ABSTRACTS

Abstracts have been categorized under various kinds and types depending upon the amount of information supplied by them. These are :

1. Indicative or Descriptive Abstracts

The indicative or descriptive abstract contains a general statement of the nature and scope of the document, excluding qualitative and quantitative data. It often consists by a single sentence or phrase explaining the form of the document. It provides clues as to whether or not information being sought is contained in the original document. As such, it is used only for documents that do not embody informative summarization, as for example, bibliographies, symposium proceedings, handbooks, state-of-the-art reviews, progress report etc. But, in some cases, while dealing with subjects of considerable complexity in order to make the abstract meaningful reference is made to some of the procedures, conclusions and results of more significant investigations.

2. Informative Abstract

A comprehensive abstract, it contains principle ideas, methods, arguments and data contained in the documents while omitting excess wordage and detail explanation. Such abstracts are thus often used in information retrieval systems, e.g. Chemical Abstracts, Biological Abstracts. Such types of abstracts are also desirable for documents reporting experimental or investigative activity or situations of a singular nature. Included are an explanation of the nature and the scope of the problem or situation, the objectives of the investigation, an account of the study or research methods, the major findings or results, conclusions and recommendations and appropriate collateral or incidental information.

3. Indicative - Informative Abstract or Mixed Abstract

Indicative-informative abstracts combine the characteristics of both. In such abstracts, less important aspects are treated indicatively, while precise information is provided for the significant aspects of the document. These abstracts communicate adequate information with economy.

4. Listing Abstract

Listing abstracts list the contents of the documents and are often used for volumes of conference proceedings, in which case they give the authors, titles, and page numbers of the individual papers. In some cases, the papers also have their own abstracts.

5. Critical Abstract

In a critical abstracts, the abstractor functions as an evaluator. For indicative and evaluative abstracts, the abstractor normally functions as an objective reporter. His opinions are carefully excluded. For critical or evaluative abstracts, the abstractor injects his opinions and analysis. The value of critical abstract depends upon the subject competence of the abstractor much more so than the other types of abstracts. Hence, extra care has to be taken in preparing critical abstracts. Example of critical abstracts is found in Applied Mechanics Review and Referativnyi Zhurnal: Mekanika.

6. Titular Abstract

The title of the document representing its contents is titular abstract. A good title is often sufficient to indicate, particularly to the experienced reader, whether the paper is of interest. This is particularly relevant to scientific documents, where the title usually indicates the subject.

7. Summary or Synopsis Abstract

This is similar to the indicative abstracts, though normally it is sufficiently long to give an outline of the whole of the work described. Many journals require authors to write a summary of their papers. These summaries are sometimes republished in certain abstracting periodicals.

8. Slanted Abstract

Abstracts are usually prepared keeping in view the users purpose, the area of research, and depth of information required. Hence, they become biased in outlook.

Ranganathan called it 'slant in abstracting'.

When an abstract is oriented to serve a special group, it is called a slanted abstract. For instance, the same document may be abstracted in the Biological Abstracts and in the Chemical Abstracts, but the abstracts in both the cases will be different, one for the biologists and other for the chemists. Similarly, an abstract may be findings oriented, giving more emphasis on the findings or results of the research reported in the paper.

9. Pseudo Abstract

Identified by T.E.R. Singer, the Pseudo Abstract is described as an abstract of a paper that has not yet been, and may never be, written. It originates from the practice of inviting speakers before professional associations to submit abstracts of their papers for publications prior to delivery of the full paper. Often, these papers are delivered extempore and may never be produced to full text. Accordingly, an abstract of this paper remains in the literature as the abstract of a paper that has never been published nor otherwise recorded.

10. Telegraphic Abstract

Abstracts written in a highly regularized form have been tried primarily for facilitating computer search through the abstracts themselves. Such abstracts have been called telegraphic because they sound like telegrams. Telegraphic abstract is a detailed index to a graphic record, which is composed of: Significant words selected from the documents; Code symbols called role indicators, which supply a context for the selected words; and Punctuation symbols, which separate and group the words and Role indicators into varied units in somewhat the same fashion as conventional punctuation does.

Telegraphic abstract is also called standardized or encoded abstract.

11. Graphic Abstract

In the field of Chemistry, where a precise language of communication is available, the Current Abstracts of Chemistry and the Index Chemicus, making full use of this language, have introduced a new type of abstract. This has been named Graphic Abstract. Instead of naming the substances and compounds, and their treatments, a graphic abstract indicates them by molecular and structural formulae.

12. Statistical or Tabular Abstract

This is used for certain specialized subjects such as thermo-dynamic properties where the emphasis is exclusively on the data. This abstract is a summary of the data presented in tabular form.

13. Highlight Abstract

This is the incomplete abstract which appears either in the table of contents or adjacent to it, serving as an appetizer.

14. Auto Abstract

Since abstracting is an expensive venture because of the amount of intellectual effort involved in it, investigations are on to replace it with mechanical effort. This idea was put forward by H.P. Luhn who suggested the use of a computer to extract abstracts from the text of the document. Sentences from the document are selected for inclusion in the abstract on the basis of the number of keywords they contain. The keywords for a particular document are determined statistically by the frequency of their appearance in the title and headings, and by their position.

In short, the Luhn process is based on two main principles:

1. Word Occurrence : which assumes that the author through his repetitive use of certain words stresses items of importance in the text.

2. Word Proximity : which assumes that the physical nearness of the words to each other in sentences is indicative of the close intellectual association of the ideas they represent.

15. Extract

The extract is a form, somewhat analogous to the abstract, for condensing document information to represent the whole. Key sentences are selected excerpted and analyzed in a logical order to present the reader with the thesis, its substantiating information and the tone or style of the document, charts, diagrams, tables and other graphic aids may be used.

Trade literature, manufacturers, specifications and reliability or evaluation data are very suitable for incorporating in the extract system. Essential information can be readily retrieved without the inter-position of documents retrieved.

STAGES OF ABSTRACTING

The process of abstracting can be discussed in the following three stages.

1. First Stage : It involves identification of key facts for which a general guidance can be given:

(a) The introductory portion of the paper or document should be read carefully. This portion usually indicates the objective of the author in writing the paper or gives the general perspective of reported study.

(b) If the document contains an author's abstract, it should be read and examined in the light of the information contained in the text.

(c) The summary and conclusion usually given at the end of the document should be read. They may indicate author's findings and should form part of the abstract.

(d) The text should then be scanned for information on the methodology of work, data and any other additional information.

2. Second Stage : It includes organization of ideas that have been selected to be included in the abstract in a sequence most helpful to the reader

(a) **Purpose :** Introductory statement should indicate the goal, objectives and aims of study (why of study)

(b) **Methodology, Techniques, Instruments :** The techniques used in attaining stated objectives.

(c) **Results :** Next comes a statement of findings reported by author.

(d) **Conclusion :** Statement dealing with interpretation or significance of the result may be included at the end.

3. Third Stage : After the key facts have been identified and the ideas organized third stage is to write the abstract in an accurate and precise manner. Certain principles may be applied to achieve best results such as :

Do's	*Don'ts*
Scan the document purposefully for key facts.	Change the meaning of original comment on or interpret the document.
Slant the abstract to your audience.	Mention earlier work.
Tell what was found	Include detailed, experimental results
Tell why the work was done apparatus	Describe details conventional
Tell how the work was done	Mention future work
Place findings early in the topical sentence	Begin abstract with stock phrases
Put details in succeeding sentences	Use questionable jargon
Place general statements last separate relatively independent subjects	Waste words by stating the obvious
Differenciate experiment from hypothesis Be informative but brief	Say the same thing two ways , Use noun-form of verbs

Be exact, concise and unambiguous	Over use of synonyms
Use short, complete sentences	Use "high - polymer adjectives"
Use short, simple, familiar words	Use a choppy, telegraphic style.
Avoid unnecessary words	
Use generic expression when possible	
Employ normal technical English	
Use direct statements (active voice)	
Describe conclusions in the present tense	
Use abbreviations sparingly	
Cite bibliographical data completely.	

USES OF ABSTRACTS

There are quite a number of uses for abstracts. Here is a list of some of them;

1. Promote Current Awareness : The scanning of all available literature on even a segment of knowledge is almost impossible today. Too much literature is available already and is further growing at a tremendous rate. Abstracts, by repackaging information into a more condensed form, faster keeping up i.e., current awareness.

2. Save Reading Time : Since an abstract is an abbreviated and accurate representation of a document contents, the reading of abstract results in net saving of time. Even more important than the reading time saved is the improved assimilation and integration of what is read.

3. Facilitate Selection : Titles as, subject paraphrases are too often uninformative, especially regarding the specific details that are vital to the selection of articles to be read. Titles also tend to be general because of the necessity for brevity. Thus, titles may be poor guides to the selection of readings. Carefully written abstracts are usually for superior to titles and to entries for use when selecting documents to be read.

4. Help to Overcome the Language Barrier : There are about 80 languages in which science and engineering reports occur, but the scientists or technologist is able to read only one or two languages. Providing abstracts in one of the more common languages, which are known, to the scientists or technologists can rectify this mismatch. In many cases, abstracts function as surrogates for the original foreign language document and in others, they lead more reliably than index entries or titles, to a translation or to a decision that a translation should be obtained.

5. Facilitate Literature Searches : Without abstracts, comprehensive. literature search would be impossible. Now a days some 60,00 to 1,00,000 periodicals are estimated for carrying the findings of scientific research. It is impossible for any individual to assemble and search this mass of literature. Without indexed abstracts, searches of such a vast mass of literature would be impossible and data would be irretrievably lost.

6. Improve Indexing Efficiency : Abstracts facilitate indexing in two ways i.e., the abstract concentrates on the indexable subjects so that indexing proceeds at two to four times the rate required **for** original documents; and elimination of the language problem enables assignment of abstracts for indexing by subjects only. This specialization improves both the quality and the rate of indexing, because the subject specialist is not required to read another language.

7. Aid in the Preparation of Reviews and Bibliographies : The preparation of articles, bibliographies, and reviews **and** extensions talks requires organization of the material used, so do acquisition and searching. Abstracts can be used to facilitate this organization. For this purpose, they can be copied, cut and pasted. Organized abstracts also facilitate the indexing bibliographies and reviews.

8. Serve as Predictive Tools : Abstracts serve as a means of predicting whether the original, full source material is worth reading or not. Further, abstracts are more convenient to arrange into related groups than is the original literature.

9. Aid Accuracy : By use of abstracts, accuracy of selection of literature to be read or translated is increased over that of the selection from titles or titles plus annotations. The additional information in the abstract increases the accuracy.

An abstract should contain enough information, which would help the subject specialists to decide whether he should read the paper in full. Thus, the abstracts should act as an appetizer. At the same time, it should include as much information as possible, so that it is unnecessary for them to read the whole paper. The techniques applied for abstracting and the stages involved in preparing abstracts call for intellect and skill on the part of the abstractor. It is not an easy job. The abstract should be simple in language; concise in form and expressive at the same time, so that the reader does not need to consult the original document in order to understand what the abstract says, otherwise the whole purpose of abstracting will be defeated.

REFERENCES

1. Borko, Harold and Bernier Charles L. *Abstracting: Concepts and Methods. New York : Academic, 1975.*
2. Guha B., *Documentation and Information - 2nd rev. ed. - Calcutta: World Press, 1983.*
3. Khanna, J.K., *Communicating Knowledge. Delhi: Research, 1996.*
4. Riaz, Muhammad, *Modern Techniques of Documentation and Information Work. Delhi: Royal, 1992.*

Part V
Information Retrieval

21

Search Strategy

Searching subsystem is one of the major subsystems of an information retrieval system. At searching stage, the users queries are received, interpreted, appropriate search statements are formulated, and the actual search (i.e. matching with the document profile or database) is conducted. All these tasks can be performed manually, or can be mechanized. The development of cheaper direct access mass storage devices, magnetic discs and drums, associated software and advancements in communication channels brought about the possibility of more dynamic searching through online. However, a user often faces difficulties in approaching an appropriate search system, especially in formulating an appropriate search statement. The cost of searching a database, whether manually or online, can be reduced significantly if an appropriate strategy for searching is followed. Search strategy provides the facility to select the optimum path for searching a file or a database.

Search Strategy-Its Pre-requisites : There are many questions, which need consideration in formulating an appropriate search statements, viz., The concepts or facets to be searched and their order; The term(s), which appropriately represents the search concept; The feature(s) of the retrieval system to be approached; and The measures to be taken in revising a search statement.

FEATURES OF SEARCH STRATEGY

Developing a good search strategy requires knowledge about the nature and organization of target database(s) and also exact need of the user. Understanding of the user's exact requirement has much impact on the actual search and retrieval process. In some cases, the user may only want some relevant items on a given topic; in this case the task of searching will be limited.

Conversely, the user may want to get all relevant items; in this case, the search must be exhaustive.

Kinds of Search : One may identify three kinds of search: High recall search; High precision search, and Brief search.

High Recall Search : When the user needs to find out all the relevant items on the stated topic.

High Precision Search : When the user needs only relevant items i.e. as less number of non-relevant items as possible.

Brief Search : When the user wants only a few relevant items as opposed to all relevant items.

STAGES OF THE SEARCH

The process of preparing and conducting a search is complex activity involving various stages

1. Pre search interview
2. Necessary Search aids
   - System manual and search aids
   - System and database newsletter
   - Vocabulary control devices and Classification schemes, dictionaries, glossaries etc.
3. Information about the query
   - Consultation of different reference sources.
   - Determination of exact requirement of the user

in terms of query as well as level of requirement e.g. urgency, restrictions regarding number, types, languages etc. of documents.

4. Whether online searching is necessary
   - Decisions regarding availability of databases on the given subject area, its coverage, cost and other related factors.
5. Choice of database governed by factors like
   - Subject coverage
   - Document coverage
   - Accessibility
6. Decision regarding system to use according to
   - Database coverage
   - Search fields
   - Search devices
   - Performance etc.
7. Analysis of query and selection of search terms through
   - Knowledge of the system and files
   - Use of reference tools
8. Planning and carrying out the search through
   - Preparation of initial profile
   - Narrowing down the search by reducing 'OR' terms and adding 'AND' terms, if necessary
   - Broadening the search by reducing the 'AND' links and increasing the 'OR' terms if necessary.
9. Obtaining results and communicating with the user
   - Using the most suitable print format
   - Getting user's responses regarding the search results.
10. Recording
    - The steps followed in the search
    - The user's responses regarding the search results.

It may be noted that one major task in the searching process relates to the coordination of terms in order to formulate the actual search statement. The result of the search depends largely on how adequately the search terms are combined. Since the beginning of mechanized information retrieval Boolean search techniques have been used widely. Major aspects of Boolean searching are introduced in the section given below:

BOOLEAN SEARCH

George Boole devised a system of symbolic logic in which he used three operators, viz.'+', '–' and '–'. All information retrieval search systems allow the users to express their queries by using these operators.

Logical product (X) or AND logic allows the searcher to specify the coincidence of two or more concepts. For example, in order to ask for information on 'computers and information retrieval' the user may formulate the search statement as (COMPUTERS) AND (INFORMATION RETRIEVAL).

(COMPUTER) AND (INFORMATION RETRIEVAL)

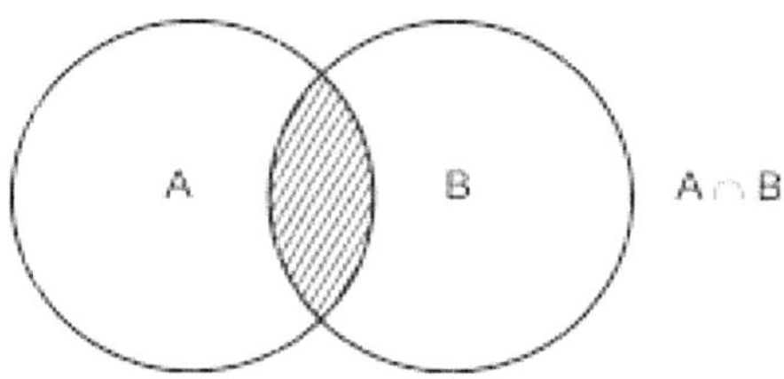

Venn Diagram for Logical Product Operator

Logical Sun or 'OR' logic allows the searcher to specify alternatives among search terms (or concepts). For example with the query statements

(COMPUTERS) OR INFORMATION RETRIEVAL

The searcher mentions that items **on** either of these two topics or both will serve the purpose.

(COMPUTER) OR (INFORMATION RETRIEVAL)

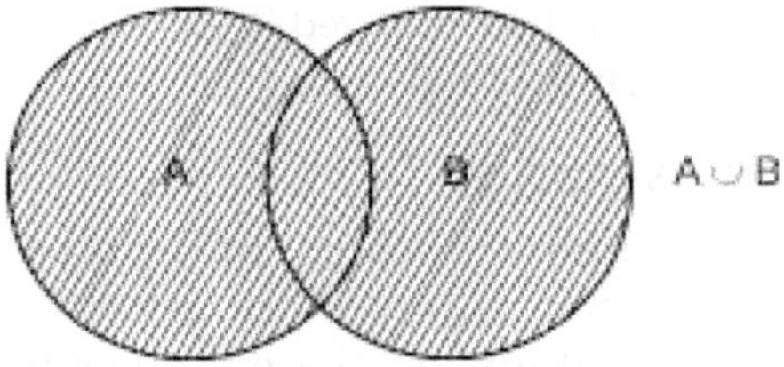

Venn Diagram for Logical Sum Operator

Logical difference or NOT logic provides facilities to exclude items from a set of items. For example, with the search statement

(INFORMATION RETRIEVAL) AND NOT (DBMS)

The user specifies his choice and thus categorically mentions his disliking for some topic in the retrieval.

(INFORMATION RETRIEVAL) AND NOT (DBMS)

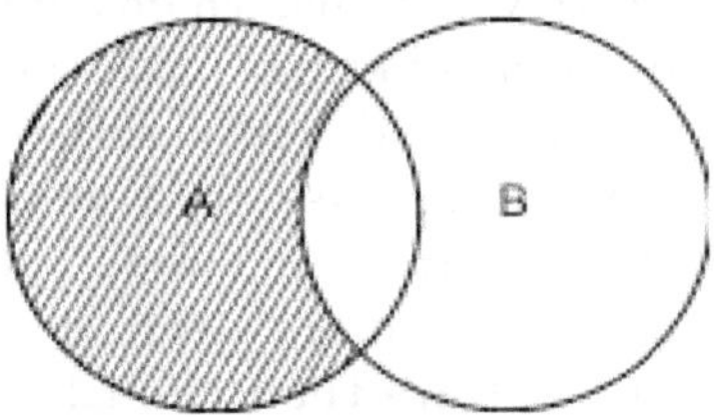

Venn Diagram for Logical Difference Operator

All these three operators may be combined in one search statement e.g. (INFORMATION RETRIEVAL) OR (INFORMATION SCIENCE) AND (ONLINE) OR (COMPUTERS) AND (DEVELOPING COUNTRIES) OR (THIRD WORLD) AND NOT (DBMS)

However, when the operators are used in combinations, the resulting search statement becomes quite complex.

LIMITATIONS OF BOOLEAN SEARCH

It has been noted that users are not able to formulate exact search statement by the combination of AND, OR, NOT operators. It has been noted that the users cannot predict exactly how many items are to be retrieved to satisfy the query. It identifies an item as relevant by finding out whether a given query term is present or not in a given record in the database. Thus, all of the retrieved items seem to be of equal importance although it is not true.

NON-BOOLEAN SEARCHES

The above shortcomings of Boolean Searches necessitated the need to pay more attention to provide facilities which would enable the end user to search in a more effective manner; resulting in the development of more sophisticated searching techniques. These include :

Best Match Searching

Also called as nearest neighbour or ranked output searching. This technique is designed to produce ranked output through the application of statistical techniques. It therefore requires a method to measure the relative importance of the retrieved items, which again requires some method of weighing of the search terms. A best match search can be implemented very efficiently using an inverted file searching technique. The user in a best match search environment can put the query in simple natural language, as in the form of a sentence. The terms representing the query and the document are then identified and measures taken to overcome variations due to spelling, synonyms, antonyms etc. The ranking is formed on the basis of similarities between the queries and each of the items in the file. This is done by the weighing scheme, which allocates numerical values to each index terms in a query or a document to indicate their relative importance. Once the terms are weighted and an initial search is carried out, the user may be asked to inspect a few retrieved documents to assess their relevance. These relevance judgments can be used for calculation of a new set of weights. This is called the relevance feedback search.

Best match searching has been widely applied in INSTRUCT (Interactive System for Teaching Retrieval Using Computational Techniques).

Merits of Best Match Searching : There is no need to represent the query terms with the help of AND, OR, NOT operators The users can simply express their query in sentence form. Users need not worry about the number of retrieved items, which are always placed in a ranked list of decreasing relevance. Thus, the user can simply choose some top-listed rather than the whole set.

Demerits : However, best match searching has certain limitations, especially in multifaceted queries, to overcome which hybrid systems have been developed which make use of both Boolean and best match search.

ON-LINE SEARCHING

Online searching refers to the process of directly interrogating computer systems to resolve particular requests for information. This search process being interactive, the user can make necessary changes in the search statement until a satisfactory result is obtained

Online searching is particularly useful when :

1. Two or more concepts must be coordinated.
2. New concepts are involved which may not have been incorporated in the indexing of printed sources but can be found in online free text searching.
3. A retrospective searches is to be carried out.

KINDS OF ONLINE SEARCH SYSTEMS

Four main types of online search systems can be identified. They are External search services; Compact disc Read Only Memory (CD-ROMs); Systems with locally stored databases; and Videotext & teletext systems.

1. External Search Services

There are four major components of an external search services :

(a) Information providers or database producers who provide database to be accessed in an online mode.

(b) Search service or host, which provides access to database and software to conduct the search.

(c) Communication links connecting the user with the host and the actual databases.

(d) Computer terminal or workstation linking the user to the service.

Example of external search services - DIALOG Information Services, USA; BLAISE, London, ESA-IRS, Italy, and ORBIT Search Service, Virgina.

2. CD-ROMs

These are high-density optical discs, capable of storing huge amount of records. Databases, which need not be updated quite frequently, or retrospective databases, are most suitable for CD-ROMs. The searching of the CD-ROM is carried out locally using a supplier search software, hence communication links are not required. The Library Association, UK is an example of an early information provider on CD-ROM, with the Library and Information Science Abstracts (LISA) on CD-ROM.

3. Locally Stored Databases

Many library and information centres have their own locally stored databases, which can be searched online. A large number of software packages like ASSASSIN, CAIRS, POLYDOC; STATUS etc. have been developed for this purpose. One particular type of in-house database is the library catalogue, online public access catalogue or OPAC, which provides facilities for library users to carry out online catalogue searches and check the availability of items required.

4. Videotext and Teletext Systems

These cover a range of systems, which use a television set, or a workstation to display computer-based information. A teletext service like CEEFAX or ORACLE in Britain involves the information being broadcast by the television.

Videotext systems like CAPTAIN in Japan, Telidon in Canada, or PRESTEL in Britain, use telephone lines to provide a two-way interactive link between the searcher and the system.

ELEMENTS OF ONLINE SEARCH

These can be split into: Searcher; Search Formulation; Input search formulation; Workstation; Link to computer system; Search software; Store of information; Retrieved items; and Printer.

The basics of an online search system are represented by the following figure:

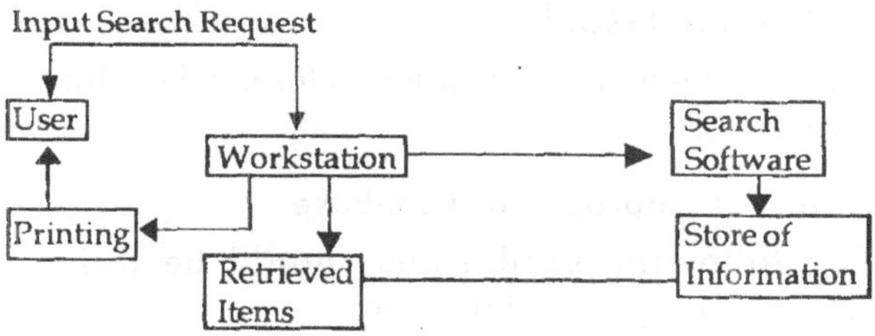

Basics of an Online Search System

MERITS OF ONLINE SEARCHING

1. The amount of time spent searching the literature is vastly reduced.
2. Searching online offers much enhanced capabilities over manual searching, by making available more access points per record.
3. The library manager is not faced with 'front-end' or 'subscription charges' for using online databases; he only pays for the time he is connected to a specific database.
4. Online access ensures complete file integrity. Since the user cannot be inconvinced by missing or misfiled issues or by the non-receipt of issues.
5. Online search results are presented in a concise and

standardized format whose detail can be predetermined by the searcher.

6. The problems of geographical location as barriers to the transfer of information are eliminated through online access particularly when the benefits of multi database searching are considered.
7. Searching databases online gives searcher much earlier access to references than when searching manually.
8. Online access makes it possible for the library or information searcher to serve more users.

ONLINE SEARCH ISSUES

There are many pre-requisites for good on-line search. These are:

(i) Selection of Appropriate Database

The following guidelines should be followed for selecting an appropriate database:

(i) Frequency of updating- the more current the information, the more acceptable it is.

(ii) Availability of documents covered by the database,

(iii) Restrictions regarding language, country of origin, form etc.

(iv) Number of primary journals included in the database,

(v) Nature of the covered documents.

(vi) Nature of the index used.

(vii) Fields or records available for searching.

(viii) Language-controlled / uncontrolled.

(ix) Costs.

(x) Overlapping of databases in the same or related systems.

(ii) Search Formulation

Serarch formulation is most demanding aspect, which

involves some intellectual process, hence it is not easy to automate it. Recent research efforts are attempting to use some sort of knowledge in developing front-end or user interfaces using expert systems and artificial intelligence.

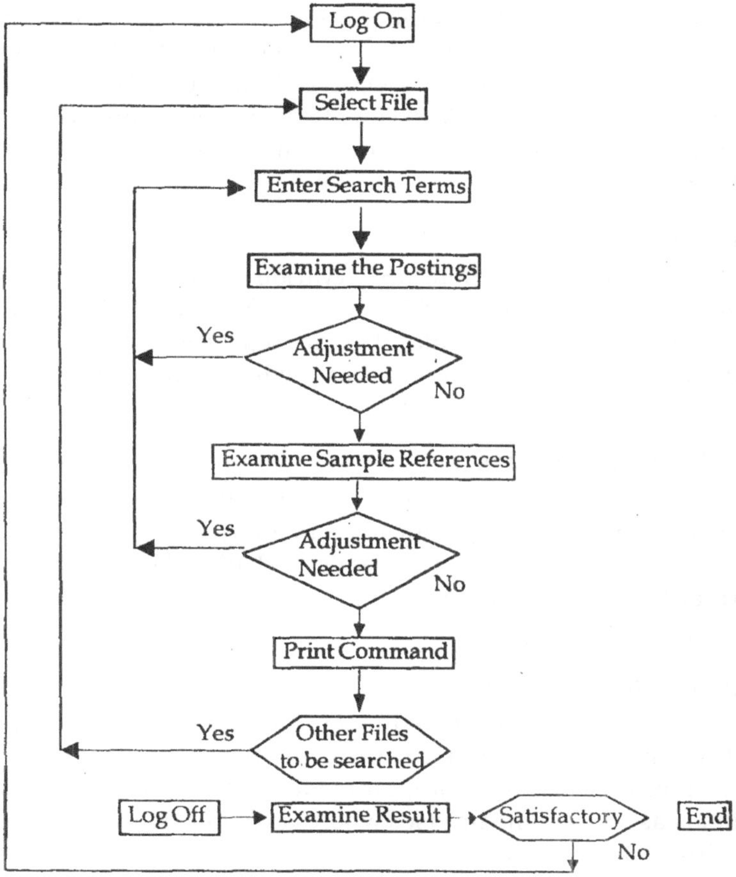

Search Operation Flow Chart

(iii) Actual Search

Even if a pre-search interview is conducted carefully, it is always best to conduct the actual search in the presence of the user, to facilitate easy communication and sort out any ambiguities on the spot.

(iv) Term Truncation

Term truncation is the most widely adopted method in online searching and it means stripping of the uncommon parts of some terms, which have some portion in common, in order to facilitate the search process. For example, the term COMPUT* includes all terms beginning with COMPUT, thus covering terms like COMPUTER, COMPUTING, COMPUTATION, COMPUTATIONAL etc. Truncation is extremely useful in searching and saves drastically on keying.

(v) Phase Searching

Some systems allow preservation of phase in the query statement. Example: Indian history, Mughal architecture etc. These systems display the appropriate section of the dictionary or thesaurus to indicate whether a given phrase is allowed in the system or not.

(vi) String Searching

This is a technique for locating a string of characters, even if it is completely embedded in a larger term. Here the searching takes place in a sequential file of bibliographic records. String searching is highly useful in case of chemical nomenclature.

(vii) Field Searching

Some systems provide facilities for searching in different fields like author, title, etc. Systems designed on the mixed dictionary concept provide a listing of the different fields as a guideline in cases where no field is marked in the initial search term.

(viii) Sequential Search

The simplest method of searching is to store the records in an array and then look up the array one by one to find out the record sought. This is called a sequential search, and is carried out by comparing each stored record in turn with an available query and retrieving appropriate data for all records whose search keys match with the query keys.

(ix) Binary Search

If the set of records is too large, then the search time becomes quite large in case of a sequential search. However, the search time can be reduced significantly by using a search procedure based on the 'divide and conquer paradigm'.

(x) Tree Search

Binary search is most commonly conducted by using a tree structure of the records. A tree structure consists of nodes or vertices containing node information together with pointers giving access to additional nodes of the tree. Only one other node called the Parents points to every node. A tree organization supports operations like searching for a record, inserting new records and deleting records.

(xi) Multi Key Search

Here, a principal key is identified and the file ordered in accordance with the values of that key. When the principal key is used as part of a search statement, the sub-section of the file corresponding to the given principal key value can then be isolated and subjected to a separate search based on the values of any secondary keys also included in the search query. A library catalogue can be considered as a multi key file, where the keys are the author, title, publisher, subject etc. Here the principal key is usually the author with the file being ordered in accordance with the author's surnames. From each record in the main file, there may be a number of pointers giving access to different secondary keys e.g., publisher. A simple file of authors and publishers can be ordered with the author's name as the principal key and a sparse index giving access to a chain of pointers for each publisher name. This type of record organization is called a multilist.

(xii) Hashing

A completely different approach to searching is provided by hashing, a method for directly referencing records in a table by doing arithmetic transformations on keys into table addresses. If we know that the keys are distinct integers from 1 to N, we can store the record with Key 1 in table position 1; which can be readily accessed with the key value. Hashing is a generalization of this trivial method for typical searching application when we don't have such specialized knowledge about the key values.

(xiii) Feedback & Reformulation

It is an instrument of responses, which is used by the recipient to inform his opinion or reactions to the information provider, usually for the services provided by the information center.

An instrument for feedback in the form of a proforma will save the time of the users. Feedback from the users are made use of for supplying the full text of references, modifying the profiles, evaluation of the references and assess various attributes of the services such as presentation, pertinence, timeless quality and document delivery services.

It is not easy to get feedback from users. However, the users should be encouraged to provide feedback. The profile of the users if necessary can be modified by information centre depending upon the feedback or response received from the user.

Despite the many technological developments during the last few years in the world of information retrieval, Boolean search technique is still in use on a large scale. Although statically based search systems like 'Best match searching' method provide better retrieval facilities, their systems yet to be adopted widely by the commercial and large retrieval systems.

REFERENCES

1. Chowdhary, G. G., *Information Retrieval System. Calcutta: IASLIC, 1994.*
2. Kent, Allen., *Information analysis and Retrieval. New York: Becker and Hayes, 1962.*

Selected Bibliography

1. Austin, Derek and Butcher, Peter, *PRECIS: A Rotated Subject Index System. British National Bibliography. London, 1969.*
2. Bhattacharya, G. *POPSI: Fundamentals and Procedure. Annual Seminar (DRTC), 12, 1975.*
3, Chakraborthy, A.R. and Chakraborthy, B., *Indexing Principles, Processes and Products. Calcutta: World Press, 1984.*
4. Chowdhury, G.G., *Information Retrieval System. Calcutta: IASLIC, 1994.*
5. Cleverland, D.B., *Introduction to Indexing and Abstracting. Littleton: Libraries Unlimited, 1983.*
6. Cleverland, D.B., *Introduction to Indexing and Abstracting. Littleton: Libraries Unlimited, 1983.*
7. Collison, Robert L., *Indexes and Indexing. London: Ernest Benn Limited, 1959.*
8. Doyle, Louren B., *Information Retrieval and Processing. Los Angeles: John Willey, 1975.*
9. Foskett, A.C., *A Guide to Personal Indexes. 2nd ed. London: Clive Bingley, 1970.*
10. Foskett, A.C., *Subject Approach to Information. London: Clive Bingley, 1982.*
11. Ghosh, S.B. and Satpathi, J.N., *Subject Indexing Systems: Concepts, Methods and Techniques. Calcutta: IASLIC, 1998.*
12. Guha, B., *Documentation and Information: Services, Techniques and Systems. Calcutta: World Press, 1983.*
13. Houghton, Bernard and Convey, *John Online Information Retrieval Systems: An Introductory Manual to Principles and Practice. London: Clive Bingley, 1984.*

14. Kemp, Alister, *Knowledge Base Retrieval Systems. London: ASLIB. 1988.*

15. Kent, A., *Information Analysis and Retrieval. New York: Becker and Haynes, 1992.*

16. Khan, M.T.M., *Information Organization and Communication. New Delhi: Ess Ess, 1997.*

17. Lancaster, F.W., *Indexing and Abstracting. London: LA, 1991.*

18. Lancaster, F.W., *Information Retrieval Systems: Characteristics, Testing and Evaluation, 2nd ed. New York: John Wilety, 1979.*

19. Luhn, H.P., *Key-Word-In-Context Index for Technical Literature. Am. Doc 11, 1960.*

20. Maltby, Arthur, *Sayers Manual of Classification for Librarians. London: Andra Deutsch,1975.*

21. Oddy, R.N. [et.al.] (ed.), *Information Retrieval Research. London: Butterworths,1981.*

22. Prashar, R.G., *Information and Its Communication. New Delhi: Medallion, 1991.*

23. Ranganathan, S.R., *Prolegomena to Library Classification, ed. 3, 1967.*

24. Ranganathan, S.R., *Subject Heading and Facet Analysis. Journal of Documentation. v. 6, 1964.*

25. Riaz, Mohammad, *Modern Techniques of Documentation and Information Work. Delhi: Royal, 1992.*

26. Rijsbergen, Van C.J., *Information Retrieval. London: Butterworths, 1979.*

27. Rowley, J.E., *Abstracting and Indexing. London: Clive Bingley, 1982.*

28. Sharp John R., *Some Fundamentals of Information Retrieval. London: Andre Deutsch Limited, 1965.*

29. Varma A.K., *Trend in Subject Indexing. Delhi: Mittal, 1984.*

30. Vickery, B.C. and Vickery A., *Information Science in Theory and Practice. London. Butterworths. 1987.*

31. Vickery, B.C., *Techniques of Information Retrieval. London: Butterworths, 1970.*

Index